# SURFER STORIES

*Tom Curren in 1981 at Rincon Cove, Santa Barbara, California. Photo by Jimmy Metyko*

# SURFER STORIES

**12 UNTOLD STORIES** BY **12 WRITERS**
ABOUT 12 OF THE **WORLD'S GREATEST SURFERS**

EDITED BY
**CLAUDIA LEBENTHAL**

A REGALO PRESS BOOK
Surfer Stories:
12 Untold Stories by 12 Writers about 12 of the World's Greatest Surfers
© 2025 by Claudia Lebenthal
All Rights Reserved

ISBN: 979-8-88845-230-1
ISBN (eBook): 979-8-88845-231-8

Cover photo: 1977 World Champion Shaun Tomson at age 14 in Makaha, Hawaii, 1969. The surfboard was shaped by surfing's first World Champion (1964), Australian Midget Farrelly.

Interior design and composition by Greg Johnson, Textbook Perfect

This is a work of nonfiction. All people, locations, events, and situations are portrayed to the best of the author's memory.

As part of the mission of Regalo Press, a donation is being made to the Surfrider Foundation, as chosen by the author. Find out more about this organization at: https://www.surfrider.org.

PUBLISHING TEAM
Founder and Publisher: Gretchen Young
Editorial Assistant: Caitlyn Limbaugh
Managing Editor: Madeline Sturgeon
Production Manager: Alana Mills
Production Editor: Rachel Paul
Associate Production Manager: Kate Harris

This book, as well as any other Regalo Press publications, may be purchased in bulk quantities at a special discounted rate. Contact orders@regalopress.com for more information.

No part of this book may be reproduced, stored in a retrieval system, or transmitted by any means without the written permission of the author and publisher.

REGALO PRESS
New York • Nashville
regalopress.com

Printed in Canada
1 2 3 4 5 6 7 8 9 10

DEDICATED TO THOSE WHO LOVE THE SPORT

*Kelly Slater in 2013 at Pipeline, Oahu, Hawaii. Photo by Brian Bielmann*

# CONTENTS

## INTRODUCTION
By Claudia Lebenthal   1

## KEEP PADDLING
Garrett McNamara by Gerry Lopez   7

## THE TALE OF A CAT WITH NINE LIVES
Gerry Lopez by Jim Kempton   25

## A HEART SHINING THROUGH DARKNESS
Rell Sunn by Karen Rinaldi   53

## LAIRD'S WAVE
Laird Hamilton by Sam George   73

## FOR THE LOVE OF DEREK HYND
Derek Hynd by Jamie Brisick   91

## I WILL
Shaun Tomson by Chris Carter   111

## WAVES OF CONSEQUENCE: KEALA KENNELLY'S REVOLUTIONARY PATH
Keala Kennelly by Liza Monroy   129

## CRY AN OCEAN
Robert "Wingnut" Weaver by Holly Peterson   151

## BETHANY HAMILTON'S PERFECT DAY
Bethany Hamilton by Captain Brett Crozier, U.S. Navy (Retired)   173

## FEBRUARY
Michael February by Selema Masekela   193

## FINDING TOM CURREN
Tom Curren by Chris Shiflett   207

## IN THE MOMENT
Kelly Slater by Shaun Tomson   237

## AFTERWORD
To Surf & Protect   257

# INTRODUCTION

Surfing has an allure, a mystique that captivates people even if they don't surf. To see the ocean rising up, cresting into a wave, curling over as a surfer rides down its face and tucks into a spiraling barrel of water is mesmerizing. Surfers make it look effortless, like something anyone can do, or at least imagine—myself included.

I dream of being inside that blue and green tunnel of water. It must be the most incredible feeling. Yes, I surf, but not very well. I am drawn to the sport as an observer, watching those surfers who have set themselves apart from the rest with an inimitable style and fearlessness.

These are twelve of their stories: twelve stories by twelve writers about twelve of the world's greatest surfers. But how do you choose just twelve surfers when there are infinitely more legends in the sport? You don't. You pick twelve writers—albeit another challenge in itself—and let them choose the surfer whose story they want to tell.

I had originally come up with a list of about twenty-five surfers. They were the obvious choices, surfers most people have heard of, like Laird Hamilton, Kelly Slater, Lisa Andersen, Duke Kahanamoku, and Shaun Tomson. Some of these are in the book; some are not. There were other surfers on my writers'

lists, two of whom I had never even heard of: Jamie Brisick wanted to write about a total madcap character, Australian surfer Derek Hynd; and Selema Masekela pitched Michael February, a young Black surfer from South Africa rising up through the rankings, whose mere presence on the pro-surfing tour would have been impossible under the apartheid regime. These two writers had personal connections to these surfers—as, in fact, did every writer in this book, whether they actually knew the surfer or not. And what stories these are!

My goal was to have a diverse group of writers from different genres: fellow surfers, famed authors, celebrities, musicians, and surf journalists, all united in their love of surfing. My first yes came from Shaun Tomson, the icon and world champion of the 1970s and '80s. Coincidentally, I had met him in East Hampton when I was a teenager. He was a family friend of some local kids. I grew up in New York City, not surfing, but for some reason he was on my radar. He asked if he could write about Kelly Slater. He wanted first dibs. Done. It was like Jack Nicklaus asking if he could write about Tiger Woods.

The next yes came from Sam George, former editor of *SURFER* magazine, the bible of the sport. He is one of the premier authorities on surfing, whose face and voice you have seen and heard in almost every surf documentary. He had put Laird Hamilton on the cover of *SURFER*'s February 2001 issue with the cover line "oh my god…" after Laird surfed what Sam called "the heaviest wave ever ridden" in Teahupoo, Tahiti. But there was a backstory that he wanted to share for the book: the story that had never been told about the week leading up to that day, and a sliding door—or should I say locked door— that put Laird on *that* wave at *that* moment in time.

Then there was Holly Peterson, the bestselling author who I happened to know was a passionate surfer. She wanted to write about Robert "Wingnut" Weaver, the longboarding star of *The Endless Summer 2*. He had accompanied her and her family on numerous surf trips as their coach, and she had traveled the world with him surfing. He had also been her guide in a turbulent time when surfing became her salvation, which she writes in her signature humorous style, in a story that is also poignantly told.

I wanted a writer from Hollywood too, a big-name star, actor, or director, as surfing has been the subject of so many great films, like *Big Wednesday*, *Point Break*, and *Blue Crush*. My cold-call emails to publicists went unanswered or received nos. But by chance I was connected by one of those nos—David Duchovny, because he didn't surf—to a Hollywood writer and producer who had actually started his career as an editor at *Surfing* magazine: Chris Carter, the creator of *The X-Files*. Chris had profiled Shaun Tomson in the 1980s at the magazine and asked if he could write about him again, forty-plus years later.

By funny coincidence, Jim Kempton, who wrote about Gerry Lopez for this book, had worked as an editor at *SURFER* when Chris was at *Surfing*. They were friends, and Jim told me he had tried to talk Chris out of going to Hollywood. "You've got the best job in the world!" he told Chris. Good thing Chris didn't listen.

And I did get a musician, a rock star no less: Foo Fighters lead guitarist and surfer Chris Shiflett, who wanted to write about Tom Curren—not just one of the sport's greatest surfers ever but a musician as well. The two also shared Santa Barbara as their hometown. Tom was notoriously elusive, and little did I know tracking him down would be such a challenge. He lived up to his billing in the aptly named film *Searching for Tom Curren*, and had me wondering who the rock star really was.

The stories of how many of these writers got "on board" are as good as some of the stories themselves. Researching surf books online, I came upon *Surf When You Can: Lessons in Life, Loyalty, and Leadership from a Maverick Navy Captain*, by retired US Navy captain—and surfer—Brett Crozier. He had famously been fired from his command of the USS *Theodore Roosevelt* in

the early days of COVID when he sounded the alarm that the disease was raging through his ship. Brett didn't have an agent, so tracking him down was also a challenge. I called a small bookshop in Northern California where he was doing a book signing and asked if they would forward an email on to his publicist. I awoke to a reply from Brett two days later with a yes, asking if he could write about Bethany Hamilton. Getting back into the water twenty-six days after a shark attack took her left arm made her as courageous to him as any combat veteran with whom he'd ever served.

I got plenty of nos too. There were people who I thought would say yes for sure, but the collection of writers and surfers I did get was destined to be. This dream team made the book so much better, broader, and important than what I had originally envisioned. The content evolved from the obvious to the diverse, with stories not just about the most famous wave riders but surfers who have become heroes out of the water as well. There are pioneers like Keala Kennelly, who is one of the best female big-wave riders, thriving on monstrous waves like Teahupoo and "Jaws." The fearlessness she has shown on forty-foot waves has been topped only by her bravery in coming out as gay at a time when that was not accepted in the surf community. Liza Monroy, an author and a surfer who had heard about the book, reached out to us, and—given a choice of surfers—asked if she could tell Keala's story.

*Surfer Stories* represents a full spectrum of surfers—Black and white, men and women, gay and straight. They are stories of life, and death, like Karen Rinaldi's story about legendary Hawaiian surfer Rell Sunn, a pioneer of women's surfing and women's health, whose diagnosis of breast cancer mirrored her own. Rell became a beacon of hope for Karen, inspiring her to return to the water and surf again as she had done.

My goal from the start was to create a book about surfing that would appeal equally to those who surf and those who don't by simply telling great human stories. They are just as much about the writer as the surfer, and I guarantee there is at least one story for each person who reads the book—who will feel a connection to one of these surfers, because the story will speak to them as personally as it did to the writer who told it. In the bigger picture, surfing is a metaphor for life, as Gerry Lopez highlights in his story about hundred-foot-wave surfer Garrett McNamara, aptly titled "Keep Paddling."

What I didn't plan are the common themes, surfers, and waves that appear in these twelve completely different stories, written in totally different styles, that somehow thread the book together with an unexpected overview of the history and culture of surfing. Thank you to all of my writers for the surfers you chose. I could not have picked a more perfect group of twelve to represent the sport.

The other thank-you I owe is to my publisher, Gretchen Young—who, though she doesn't surf, showed as much passion and enthusiasm for the sport and this book as I have, and the same dogged pursuit of excellence.

And by the way, had I been asked to write a story for this book, I would have chosen four-time world champion Lisa Andersen. She was the first woman on the cover of *SURFER* magazine, the 1996 "Photo Annual" issue no less. The cover line read, "Lisa Andersen surfs better than you." I met Lisa as an editor at Conde Nast's *Sports for Women* magazine in 1997, when I was staying at the Roxy House on Oahu's North Shore during the Roxy Quiksilver Pro. One day I ended up "caddying" for Lisa as she walked down to the beach for the contest. As people turned to look at her, they glanced over at the "surfer" next to her carrying one of her boards…and for a fleeting moment I knew what it felt like to be one of the twelve in this book.

—*Claudia Lebenthal*
*New York City, March 2024*

*Garrett McNamara in 2012 at La Jolla Reefs, San Diego, California. Photo by Ian O'Roarty*

# 1.

# GARRETT McNAMARA

## By Gerry Lopez

*"Getting the ski into the water that morning at the tiny boat ramp in Maliko Gulch, the closest launch to Jaws, had been completely challenging, the surf surge on the verge of swamping the truck and trailer. The takeout no less so, but the distraction was welcome as Garrett's mind buzzed with the thoughts of their performance, second-guessing each decision over the course of the day until it began to make him crazy. Somewhere along the way, one of the event volunteers informed him and Rodrigo that they won. Garrett remembers walking away from everyone, thinking about all the hard work, sacrifices, emotions, and everything else he'd gone through to reach this moment. He called his wife and burst into tears."*

GARRETT MCNAMARA IS ONE OF THE TOP PROFESSIONAL BIG-WAVE SURFERS, who gained worldwide recognition in the 2021 HBO docuseries *100 Foot Wave*, about the discovery and conquest of the world's biggest wave in Nazaré, Portugal. But years before, there had been another big wave and another life-changing ride at the first ever tow-in contest at "Jaws," in Maui, that would establish McNamara as one of the big names in big-wave surfing. A legendary surfer and friend, Gerry Lopez puts us on the waves with Garrett McNamara in "Keep Padding," a story about his unrelenting perseverance to keep surfing.

# KEEP PADDLING

In order to catch a wave, one must be in the right position. That position is a function of many things, because in a wide-open ocean, there aren't exactly signposts. And the waves come on their own schedule as well. The surfer waits, trying to be exactly where he thinks that next wave will be.

Where waves come from is another subject in itself, but let's take a quick look at it. Waves come from wind and can travel thousands of miles before getting to where that surfer is waiting. Depending on the time of year, a little weather slips off the Siberian coast or maybe starts up along the "Roaring Forties" latitudes in the Southern Hemisphere. Generally, we are talking about an area of low barometric pressure, although surf can also come from a high-pressure cell as well. For now, let's talk about a depression in the North Pacific. The air is cool, and as it encounters the warmer water, it begins to spin counterclockwise. It creates energy as it spins, which makes it spin faster, and the winds around its center become stronger.

As this wind blows across the surface of the sea, it forms ripples moving in the same direction. There is a transfer of energy from the air into the water. As the ripples continue their forward motion, the front-runners begin to run out of energy and slow down. The ripple behind catches up, and they blend together, combining their energy. This continues, with the waves behind reinforcing the slowing waves ahead, their energy consolidating. The most interesting thing about waves is that the water doesn't move; it is the energy that moves through the water.

As the reinforcement continues, the swells spread apart and travel together in "sets" to conserve energy. This spread is called the wave interval, or wave period, and is a more important indicator of the strength of the swell than the actual wave height. The stronger the swell, the farther apart the waves travel and the deeper into the water the energy goes. Finally, the waves approach the waiting surfer.

When swell energy runs across an outer reef or some shallow area offshore, it humps up for just an instant before sinking back down as it heads toward shore. If the surfer misses that momentary glimpse of the approaching set, he might realize too late that it's bigger than any others that day. He might also realize he's out of position and, with a terrible sinking feeling, that he is too far inside for where these waves will break…and there isn't enough time to do anything about it. This is a circumstance called "getting caught inside," and while it is a common occurrence, it is always unwelcome. Being out of position means not only that he won't be able to ride any of the waves but, in fact, they will "ride" him. In big surf, this is a terrifying experience right from that moment of realization throughout the tremendous and often dangerous pummeling to come, the extent of which is a function of how many waves are in the set. Anyone who has been in a situation where they were unable to breathe for whatever reason has a tiny idea of what it's like to be trapped underwater by pounding surf, unable to come to the surface.

Now, a surfer has several options when this happens. He can do nothing, which doesn't do any good, or he can panic, which is worse. By doing nothing, he will usually just get washed back to shore, where he will have to start all over again. Panicking may mean swallowing some water and some brief moments of terror. But if he understands what is about to happen, relaxes as much as he can to conserve energy, keeps his composure, holds position, and continues to paddle, he will lose some ground but be in a good position when the set ends. These wave sets are followed by a period of calm called a lull. During the lull, the surfer who kept his cool will be better prepared for the next set. It is from many personal experiences with exactly this situation that I have adopted a mantra that has served me well: "Keep paddling."

This is why surfing is such a good metaphor for life. Life doesn't hold still for us, and if we don't move with it, life passes us by. Surfing teaches us to go with the flow smoothly and to be in the moment spontaneously. In this way, we get the most out of the wave as well as out of life. When we find ourselves caught inside, the best thing we can do is to keep paddling, in both a figurative and a literal sense.

One surfer who has done one of the best jobs at figuring out different ways to keep paddling is Garrett McNamara. I've known him for a long time and watched as he and his younger brother, Liam, started their professional careers on the North Shore—definitely the most challenging place to do that. Both were great surfers from the beginning, big on skill, determination, and smarts. Together they pulled it off, becoming sponsored professional surfers, paid to go surfing. This is the zenith for most surfers, but unless they are at least moderately successful at surfing in contests, their shelf life is limited. Neither brother excelled in this rarefied aspect of the sport, but not many do. Talent will take you only so far in surfing…well, maybe in anything, for that matter.

Liam enjoyed a bit more success in his pro career through sheer determination and by virtue of the fact that most of his surfing happened at a spot that was gaining increasingly more recognition: the "Pipeline" on Oahu.

It's a wave I know very well, having spent much of my own career surfing it. Although first surfed in 1961, this spot—unlike the other North Shore big wave breaks of Sunset Beach, Waimea Bay, Laniakea, and Haleiwa—was shunned by surfers because of the treacherous nature of how the wave broke. Eventually, however, it was thrust into the world's limelight. The waves were a combination of beautiful, dangerous, and extremely challenging to ride, which produced brilliant and mesmerizing images and footage that reached out far beyond the surfing world. Garrett didn't have the chops when it came to riding the Pipeline, and watched as Liam kept getting paychecks while his own sponsorships dried up.

Garrett wasn't about to surrender. He had opened a surf shop, thinking that might pay off, but soon realized that being a storekeeper was seriously cutting into his surf time. That plus a small penchant for partying—a daily occurrence on the North Shore—wasn't helping his situation either. Most surfers live wild in their twenties, but when their thirties come around, usually there's a family and/or bigger responsibilities, so priorities begin to change. Even with a wife and family, Garrett was still determined to continue to "paddle out." Throwing in the towel was nowhere in his mindset. One aspect of surfing that he had gravitated to was riding big waves, and it had become a passion.

In August 2001, Garrett decided to focus all his attention on big waves, and zeroed that focus in on winning the Eddie Aikau Big Wave Invitational and the Jaws Tow-In World Cup. At thirty-five years old, when most surfers are usually thinking that their professional careers are winding down, Garrett still had some big dreams. He made a road map, listing everything he could think of that would help him reach these goals. It was a business plan for his life, a blueprint for success that would serve him well going forward. Both of his dream events, the Eddie and Jaws Tow-In, were invitational. He overcame that first hurdle when he received an invite to the Eddie…but as an alternate. The Jaws invite was easier, since Garrett already had a relationship with the event sponsor, a company from Brazil called Bad Boy.

It was in the first week of January 2002 that a strong storm in the far North Pacific flexing its muscles made the waves rolling into Hawaii big enough for these contests. Both events were called on for the same time, and a big decision for Garrett arose: Which one? As seventh alternate for the Eddie, it was not likely he would make it. The Eddie was, after all, the most prestigious big-wave event in the history of surfing. Not much would keep any of the invited surfers from paddling out.

With that in mind, Garrett went to Maui for the Jaws contest. This tow-in contest was the first of its kind, and tow-in surfing at the time was a very new and highly specialized method for riding big surf. It had been tried off and on since the 1970s, as far as I recall. The first really successful foray was Laird Hamilton, Buzzy Kerbox, and Darrick Doerner using Buzzy's Zodiac boat and a ski rope to pull each other in on a big day at Outside Backyards, the spot next to Sunset that will hold its shape when Sunset is closed out. Their success led to more attempts at various outer reef North Shore spots. The Zodiac was a decent tow vehicle, but it was a boat with an outboard motor and somewhat limited in the surf zone, especially with a surfer on the end of a tow rope.

The North Shore lifeguards had been having a lot of success with the new bigger jet skis rescuing people out in the breaking wave zones. Filmmaker Bruce Brown, director of the famed *The Endless Summer*, had heard about the tow-in surfing and wanted to include it in his new film, *The Endless Summer II*. I had told them about the big wave on Maui outside Peahi that had never been surfed. Realizing a jet ski would be greatly superior to the Zodiac as the tow-in vehicle, Bruce bought one and filmed Laird, Darrick, and Buzzy surfing on the specialized tow-in boards at the Peahi spot, aka "Jaws".… The rest is history.

*Garrett McNamara in 2013 in Nazare, Portugal. Photo by Tó Mané*

Garrett had partnered with Brazilian Rodrigo Resende for the Jaws event. In tow-in surfing, two surfers partner up; one drives the jet ski while the other surfs. For the contest, the first surfer rides three waves, then the partners switch off for the next surfer to get his three waves. Rodrigo would be in the water first, with Garrett driving the ski. They were doing fine in the first heat until Rodrigo went down attempting a deep tube. Garrett zoomed in to rescue Rodrigo, but he was late, as Rodrigo didn't come up until the next wave was almost on him. These are very big waves, thirty to forty feet high, breaking in relatively shallow water, only twenty-five to thirty feet deep. The turbulence was tremendous, worse than in any other spot. Garrett knew in an instant that he was in trouble. The propulsion system of a jet ski works by pushing a high-powered jet of water, sucking the water in one end with an impeller that forces it out through a smaller nozzle on the back to power the ski and allow steering. But in whitewater, which is quite agitated and aerated, water is not pulled into the system. There is no action, and therefore no reaction. In other words, nothing happens; the ski doesn't go.

Garrett's rescue attempt was directly in front of twenty-plus feet of whitewater. The ski cavitated in the foamy water, the looming mountain of the breaking wave bearing down on them. Both realized what was happening. Rodrigo did the only thing he could think of. Knowing he was out of breath from the terrific pounding he'd just taken, but hoping to save the ski so Garrett could come back and get him, he pushed off the back of the jet ski's rescue sled and shoved the ski away. Rodrigo slid beneath the surface, but an avalanche of whitewater hit the ski, flinging it twenty feet into the air.

The owner of the ski, Garrett's friend Roy Patterson, had tricked it out: cool sound system, rod holders for fishing, and foot straps just like on the tow boards, in which Garrett had his feet firmly secured. Somehow, by the grace of God, after he was flung up, he stayed centered on the ski. It came back down, landed flat, and gassing it with all his might, he managed to escape the torrent and survive what easily could have been the end of the ski—and their day. Rodrigo, meanwhile, was pulled from the whitewater by another ski.

Now it was Garrett's turn on the rope. But with the drama and emotions of that near-miss moment, he was indecisive on his first wave. Setting up for the backdoor tube, instead of pulling in, he pulled out…chickened out… and had to deal with the letdown from that. Surfing is extremely demanding physically, but it may be even more so mentally, especially in big waves. When the surfer is paddling, constant maneuvering for position is required to be in the right place at the perfect moment, all of it happening moment by moment, attention totally focused on each moment—no moments open for idle thoughts. With the tow rope, however, the jet ski driver does much of the positioning for his rider. There are times when the surfer is just hanging on to the handle, maybe thinking about how he blew the last wave. Weak, negative thoughts can easily sap his strength and focus. Garrett had been here too many times before. He knew what he had to do: steer his thinking back to more powerful, positive thoughts and the job at hand.

Garrett gets three waves. Each one builds his confidence for the next. And then on the last one, right at the very last seconds of the heat, Garrett puts it all together. It's not the biggest wave, but he fades deep, comes hard off the bottom, snaps a sharp cutback under the lip, and rides it like he owns the place… just *so* smooth, confident, and composed.

Getting the ski into the water that morning at the tiny boat ramp in Maliko Gulch, the closest launch to Jaws, had been completely challenging, the surf surge on the verge of swamping the truck and trailer. The takeout was no less so, but the distraction was welcome as Garrett's mind buzzed with the thoughts of their performance, second-guessing each decision over the course of the day until it began to make him crazy. Somewhere along the way, one of the event volunteers informed him and Rodrigo that they had won. Garrett remembers walking away from everyone, thinking about all the hard work, sacrifices, emotions, and everything else he'd gone through to reach this moment. He called his wife and burst into tears.

New doors started to open for Garrett after the Jaws win. Lowell Hussey, a brilliant marketing executive and one-time senior vice president of marketing and production at Time Warner, got in touch and helped Garrett see himself in a new light. A typical sponsored surfer riding for one of the surf industry companies, he explained, had a shelf life—an expiration date that was based entirely on the next younger, better surfer to come along. The only way to extend that shelf life was to become irreplaceable, and that was a function of being distinct. His idea was to create an image for Garrett McNamara as a big-wave hellman known as the "Hound of the Sea" (the Celtic meaning of the name McNamara).

Having grown up on the North Shore with all the local guys, this idea was as much an anathema to him as it was to them. Local surfers did not toot their own horns. If they were good enough, others did it for them. Garrett did not like this idea, but Lowell explained how advertising himself was the only way that he would be able to continue surfing in the manner he needed to stay on top of his game.

Garrett McNamara, in his mid-thirties, his surf sponsorships all gone, his career as a professional surfer languishing, was on the verge of slipping into oblivion. But he didn't think about giving up. He realized Lowell was right and paddled hard in this new direction. Suddenly, he finds himself as a household name, recognized by people and in places he never thought possible.

In the spring of 2010, Garrett took a call from old friend, Izzy Paskowitz. Izzy and his wife, Danielle, had one of their Surfers Healing surf camps for autistic kids going on in Puerto Rico and asked Garrett to come help, something he had done several times in the past. It turned out to be one of the most serendipitous moments of not only Garrett's life but, as it turned out, the life of a woman he met there named Nicole. It was as though destiny brought them together. Both realized that something deeper was happening from the moment they saw each other across a crowded room. Now divorced from his first wife, they became an item. Nicole was the support Garrett needed in the business Lowell had helped him start, GMac, and in what was now his job of chasing big waves all over the globe.

By chance, Nicole found an old email from a Portuguese surfer named Dino Casimiro talking about a wave in a little fishing village called Nazaré in Portugal. When Garrett expressed interest, Nicole followed up, and the next thing they knew, they were on a plane to Portugal.

They arrived in Lisbon in November 2010, on a stormy day, and drove an hour north to Nazaré. They headed straight to the historic village lighthouse, built in 1903. From there, Garrett saw some of the biggest waves he'd ever seen in his life. He and Nicole met with a couple of young guys from the town who worked for the mayor of Nazaré. Paulo "Pitbull" Salvador was a local bodyboarder who also had a surf school. Pedro Pisco didn't surf, but he knew a big wave when he saw one. Even though neither of the two guys had surfed the big waves there, it had been their idea to invite a respected big-wave surfer to come see if their wave held any possibilities for holding a big-wave event. Garrett was looking for a hundred-foot wave to ride, so their goals seem to align. Nazaré was an old fishing town, but it was fished out, and the big waves were a constant danger to the villagers more than anything else. But for Garrett, these waves might be just what he had been searching for.

Garrett realized right away that here, like on the North Shore of Oahu, the big winter swells aim straight at Nazaré. With the help of the Portuguese Navy, he found that this wave's energy channeled along a three-mile-deep undersea trench for almost one hundred miles, shoaling a half mile from shore, finally thrusting the water upward into enormous waves. But just getting in position to ride one, to "paddle out," would be a whole challenge in itself. This was like a gigantic beach-break type of wave, with fast-moving and shifting peaks, tricky to line up, and very unpredictable on top of being huge and powerful. They spent a month there in the little town, getting to know the people, understanding the ocean topography, recruiting a support team, and arranging all the special permits necessary from the Navy for Garrett to begin his campaign to ride this crazy wave.

By the next winter, in 2011, Garrett was ready to go. On October 31, the first big swell arrived. While now forty-four years old, Garrett was in top shape, fully prepared, and eager to get after it. He'd dug up two jet skis, well used but better than nothing. He'd recruited Irish big-wave surfer Al Mennie and English charger Andrew Cotton as tow partners, together with Nicole's brother, C. J. Macias. They spent the entire first day tow-surfing into thirty- to forty-foot waves, having a great time until the last wave, when Al lost his board on a wipeout. Garrett raced in to get him, only to be caught inside a very large wave that the tired old jet ski couldn't quite get over, and went backward over the falls. But Andrew was in position on the other ski, coming in to pull both Al and Garrett out.

The next day, Garrett, a little worse for wear, elected to drive instead of surf. He puts the boys into wave after wave until they are finally surfed out and ready to call it quits…but not before Garrett takes at least one wave for himself. Nicole is spotting from the top of the lighthouse while Garrett relieves himself before he jumps on the rope. She calls on the walkie-talkie that she sees a big set coming. Garrett rushes to haul up his wetsuit from around his ankles, then grabs the rope and gets ready. Nicole calls them into the third wave of the set, and it's big…easily the biggest one yet. The drop is endless.

Garrett is hoping for a tube, but that doesn't quite happen—still, it's a nice drop. As he pulls out on the shoulder to where Andrew waits, he jumps on the sled and yells to put him in deeper on the next one. But Nicole comes on the walkie-talkie, says it's time to go in, and that's the end of it. Or so it seemed…

A few days later, a picture of Garrett riding this last wave has gone viral around the world. While Garrett doesn't think it's anything special, the rest of the world sure does, calling it a ninety-foot world-record wave. Wave measurement is an arbitrary and inexact science. A surfer in Hawaii might call a particular wave ten feet, while a surfer coming from California or Australia might say that same wave is fifteen feet. A surfer from the East Coast could call it a twenty-foot face. Even to get a general agreement of whether the wave is overhead or not is asking a lot. After twenty feet, it's anybody's guess, and that is really all it is—a guess. Ninety feet is off the charts. That Garrett's wave was maybe the biggest ever ridden is probably the most accurate thing to be said about it.

Nazaré elevated Garrett's career far beyond his wildest dreams. HBO did a television series called *100 Foot Wave*, about his dream of riding a one-hundred-foot wave, plus Nazaré and the whole story behind it. People who never surfed or even knew anything about surfing knew who he was. In 2022, the show received *two* Primetime Emmy awards.

I think the most beautiful part of this whole story is the relationship Garrett and Nicole forged with the town of Nazaré, single-handedly starting the ball rolling to put this little place into the world's consciousness—and the fact that they both decided to tie the knot there, getting married on November 22, 2012, at the top of the lighthouse that they'd helped to make famous. Then there were the friendships—not only with the Portuguese but with the entire European surf community—that developed during this process. Garrett became a sports hero, a legend, at the age of forty-five no less. And of course, there is the wave that Garrett and Nicole made world-famous, and that special bond they both have with it. Nazaré will forever be a part of them.

Garrett is now well into his fifties, but once a charger, always a charger. He and Nicole have three children. He has always been and will continue to be a controversial character in the world of surfing, but perhaps, that is his fate. Whereas Laird Hamilton approached big-wave surfing with the intention to live to surf another day, Garrett's attitude was more of a do-or-die approach—he wasn't afraid to put all his marbles on the line if that's what it took…and he did it continually, putting himself into situations and places where most, knowing the awesome power of the sea, would wisely back away. Garrett, with that characteristic gleam in his eye, charged right in. Looking at his whirlwind career—the many times he got caught inside, literally and figuratively, got pounded by the waves that broke his bones but never his spirit, and had to paddle out once again—I'd have to say that no one has done it better.

The surf will come up at the big waves of Nazaré or the Cortes Bank or Jaws or Mavericks or Teahupoo or close to Garrett's home in Waimea. Garrett will feel their call to come play, and he will…

Keep paddling…keep surfing.

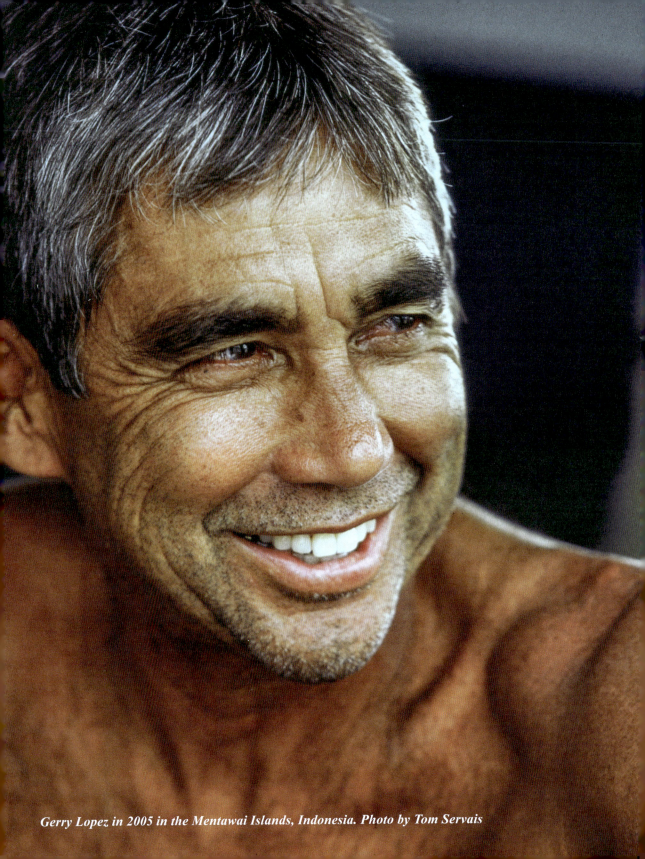

*Gerry Lopez in 2005 in the Mentawai Islands, Indonesia. Photo by Tom Servais*

# 2.

## GERRY LOPEZ

### By Jim Kempton

*"It was not always a cakewalk, however. In fact, Gerry truly did have a relatively unspectacular surf career in his early years. And some serious bumps in the road: he had numerous injuries, including a fin slicing through his buttocks that nearly crippled him. His flourishing surf shop burned down. His dream business failed. So how did he get to this place—nearly fifty years after the apex of his celebrity— of being the world's most revered surfer?"*

Gerry Lopez's longtime friend Jim Kempton, former editor and publisher of *SURFER* magazine and author, tells us how, on the evening of the California Surf Museum's Annual Gala Fundraiser where Lopez is being honored. Lopez is one of the most idolized surfers of his generation, a legendary wave rider who came of age in the 1970s and continues to surf with an inimitable flair today. He made his mark on the famous Banzai Pipeline on Oahu's North Shore with a laid-back style so cool, he made riding one of the world's most dangerous waves look effortless.

Kempton interweaves the highlights of Lopez's career with the events of the evening, bringing past and present together in nine parts about the nine lives of Gerry Lopez.

# THE TALE OF A CAT WITH NINE LIVES

### Life #1. The Mystery Inside the Enigma

In the fading light of late autumn, the patio at the Cape Rey Resort looks out across the Pacific Coast Highway and Carlsbad State Beach to the orange sun dropping low toward the sea. The Southern California breeze is just enough to cool the crowded terrace, where several hundred revelers are attending the California Surf Museum's Annual Gala Fundraiser, one of surfing culture's touchstone events. The crowd meshes a large swath of guests between the outdoor mahogany bar and the silent auction room filled with a kaleidoscope of offerings. Aging legends mix with board sport industry moguls, film directors, World Tour surfing pros, museum members, and the dedicated surfers who have come to experience being in the same room with the iconic characters being honored with the Silver Surfer Award later in the evening. Every table in the ballroom adjoining the outdoor terrace has been sold. And there is one person they have *all* come to see.

The honorees include USA surfing champion and Women's International Surfing Association founder Jericho Poppler, a pioneer of women's surfing and a character whose energy is impossible to contain. Alongside her is another

vivacious and indefatigable character, Argentine surfer Fernando Aguerre, proponent of a twenty-year effort to bring surfing to the Olympic Games. And last, there is a quiet, compact, charismatic enigma named Gerry Lopez. This is the man the paying guests are all waiting to hear later in the evening.

Few figures in sports history immediately bring to mind an unforgettable image of matchless poetic grace: Jackie Robinson's iconic base-stealing hook-slide at home plate in the World Series at Yankee Stadium. Billie Jean King drilling a forehand stroke past Bobby Riggs in the Battle of the Sexes at the Houston Astrodome. Mikhail Baryshnikov executing a perfect cabriole at New York's Carnegie Hall. Tom Brady launching a perfect spiral touchdown into the end zone at Gillette Field. Duke Kahanamoku breaking the world 100 meter swimming record by 4.6 seconds at the Olympic trials in Honolulu Harbor. Michael Jordan's airborne catapult across the stratosphere slam-dunking a ball at Chicago Stadium.… And Gerry Lopez's effortless elegance slipping behind a curtain of water in the Pipeline Masters on the North Shore of Oahu.

Those pictures of the Zen master, burned into the minds of surfers (and surf observers everywhere), are nearly all that most remember of the man. His reply, "It's a cakewalk," when asked about riding the most dangerous wave in the world, is perhaps the most well-known quote in surfing.

It is the story that everyone in surfing knows. *Or at least thinks they know.* But those images are outside of the persona, not inside it. They are, in reality, only the *surface* reflections of a very deep well.

"It's a riddle wrapped in a mystery inside an enigma…" Winston Churchill used this phrase to describe a situation that was difficult to comprehend. And no phrase might be better to encapsulate the aura Gerry projects.

Gerry will, of course, be the first to dismiss this. "I'm not special," he tells me. "I was a spaz as a kid and a kook in high school. I mean, at five-foot-eight and one hundred forty pounds, I wasn't going to be a fullback. Surfing kind of fit my limitations."

I've known Gerry since at least 1977, and whether he denies it or not, he carries a mystique about him that no surfer, save Miki Dora, has ever equaled. The man you meet has a way of being "strategic and disarming," says Matt Warshaw. Matt should know—he literally wrote the book *The Encyclopedia of Surfing*.

"Lopez—and I say this with the utmost respect—is incredibly calculating and shrewd," Matt says. "You only ever see what he wants you to see, when and where he wants you to see it. Which makes him, in this live-streaming tell-everything age, all the more attractive. He is," Matt concludes, "the last mysterious man in surfing."

The public image of Gerry Lopez—the shy, self-effacing, humble Hawaiian soul monster…the surf god with the Midas touch, turning everything that grazed his perfectly positioned fingers into gold—has always seemed too good to be true. For anyone with Gerry's fame, there are always rumors, stories; instances where tactics and decisions could be considered suspect.

I had always heard he was ruthless in the takeoff zone, burning other surfers on waves, especially at Pipeline. That has been confirmed by many of my close friends who've surfed Pipe.

When his partners at surfboard maker Lightning Bolt became entangled in a corporate power struggle, other parties in the imbroglio told me that he had sold his shares to the highest bidder, burned the guys who had brought the opportunity to him originally, and left his partner Jack Shipley hanging out to dry.

I wanted to explore these questions even if the evidence put a blemish on the sacred Gerry Lopez chronicle that had been slowly turned into gospel. Certainly there is more than meets the eye. But first let's meet the eye.

## *Life #2. Meeting the Eye*

To say Gerry Lopez is a surfer is akin to saying Leonardo da Vinci is a painter. Beyond his painting genius, da Vinci was a master sculptor, architect, writer, and theorist—and a pioneer of his world. I'm not comparing Gerry to da Vinci, of course. *But*…in the watercolors of waves, Gerry's lines and form are matchless. Yet, while his style on a liquid canvas is what he is most famous for, Gerry is a master surfboard shaper who began designing his own boards back in the late 1960s. His trademark red-and-yellow Pipeline Guns shaped for that wave are considered the refined designs that made his exceptionally graceful approach possible. *Surfing* magazine named him "Shaper of the Year 2002." Decades later, his foam sculptures are still in high demand and at the top of his field.

Although not an architect per se, Gerry bought the lot on the public entrance to Pipeline, and with his friend and business partner John Porter designed a three-story abode from the ground up. Lopez State Park, or the "Pipeline Hilton," was by far the most recognizable structure on the North Shore. And an invitation into the compound was *very* coveted exclusive access.

The decks of the house were like private box seats to spectacular performances on the Pipeline stage. Jeff Divine (the photographic chronicler of the 1970s) not only documented the surf action on display at this outdoor theater in the round, but also captured the top surfers on the North Shore in an annual front yard shot. It became a historical record of the season, commissioned by *SURFER* magazine each year during Gerry's reign.

"It made perfect sense that Gerry bought the land and built that house," Jeff once told me. "He was the king, and he got his throne."

Gerry also was a writer, a columnist at the *Honolulu-Star Advertiser*. Between the summer of 1969 and the spring of 1971, he wrote close to fifty columns on the emerging surf culture under the moniker "Gerry Ken Lopez, Advertiser Surfing Writer." Thirty-seven years later, in 2008, he finished writing *Surf Is Where You Find It*, a collection of stories about his lifetime of surfing and, more interestingly, the lessons learned from wave riding.

Remarkable for a top athlete in his field, Gerry wrote a number of articles for *SURFER* magazine—referred to at the time as the bible of surfing. One piece was a seminal essay on style titled "Attitude Dancing." Another one I commissioned from him during my stint as editor at *SURFER*. Written by hand in his unique personal calligraphy, it was interesting in both content and graphic layout—among the best pieces the magazine produced in its venerable six decades. It was a notable piece of travel writing—a firsthand account of the fabled surf spot at Grajagan in Indonesia, known informally as G-Land.

That recalls another feat Gerry can claim—pioneer. Besides pioneering the deep-tube-riding possibilities at Pipe, he was an early explorer of Indonesia's remote jungle surf spots. Although Gerry was certainly not the first person to discover G-Land, his presence there pioneered the world's best lefthand point break, where tigers still roamed the beach at night.

Gerry is also a practicing theorist—a lifelong devotee of a style of yoga that incorporates a complete philosophy of life.

OK, so we can't compare Gerry to a figure like da Vinci, who changed the universe. But in the smaller world of wave riders, Gerry Lopez may just be a Renaissance man for all seasons.

It was *not* always a cakewalk, however. In fact, Gerry truly did have a relatively unspectacular surf career in his early years. And some serious bumps in

the road: he had numerous injuries, including a fin slicing through his buttocks that nearly crippled him. His flourishing surf shop burned down. His dream business failed. So how did he get to this place—nearly fifty years after the apex of his celebrity—of being the world's most revered surfer?

### Life #3. Taking Off

As the attendees of the Surf Museum gala arrive in droves and the lines at the bar grow long, a solitary figure sits in front of a film camera and an interviewer. Concealed behind the resort's lush plantings, the star of the evening's festivities goes unnoticed by the crowd.

I'd had Gerry slip out of his room and quietly down the back hallway to prevent the usual ruckus whenever he appears in public. Sometimes, when there are as many people as there are tonight, it can turn into an uncomfortable madhouse.

When I first invited Gerry to be a recipient of the Silver Surfer Award, he didn't respond immediately. *Probably too busy*, I thought. He was living in Bend, Oregon—a long way to travel. But then I arrived on Oahu for the winter season to install a Pipeline Masters exhibit at the Turtle Bay Resort. Sometime during the first few days of each season, every surfer on the North Shore comes through the hotel lobby. Gerry strolled in with his friend George Kam, and we exchanged friendly greetings while I teetered on a ladder attaching an exhibit surfboard to the wall. Still no mention of the gala attendance.

Later in the week, when Gerry and George came by Billabong's Off the Wall beach house for a quick interview with the contest sponsors, George spoke to me: "Gerry told me 'I think Jim really needs this one. He's calling in a chip. I think I need to go to the gala.'" What I didn't know was that, when Gerry decided to attend, he also decided to build a hand-shaped surfboard to donate to our auction fundraiser. But as soon as George told me, I knew it would be the highest-selling item of the night.

For years, people have said to me, "Can you ask Gerry to do you a big favor for us? You are good friends with him, right?"

I hesitate before answering, but my response is almost always the same:

"Yes, we are friends. But part of that long relationship is that I *don't* ask him for something every time a request comes down the line."

Now Gerry is here, shadowed from the crowd but graciously giving one more interview to yet another media group. Although not in a Lotus position, his posture is always poised. He speaks with a steady, low-key cadence—a quiet sureness that comes from having studied what makes him happy. And he has spent his life living the way he wants to.

Watching him interact with the camera displays his innate instincts—not just in the physical sense but in the pivotal decisions he has made on life's journey.

He talks about his early equipment, his influences, and his upbringing. He begins by reflecting on the first board he shaped himself for Pipeline. It was dubbed the "Coral Cruiser."

"I knew the great Pipe riders before me were held back by their equipment," he explains. "I looked at the early Waimea guns built for speed and thought, 'Maybe I should take a shot at this type of design.'" The moment he caught his first wave, he realized, "I think I've got something here."

Indeed he did. The board not only changed Gerry's surfing; it changed the way surfers thought about surfing big, hollow, intense waves. His style embodied (to steal a great line from Hemingway) grace under pressure.

Rory Russell, Gerry's longtime friend and the undisputed second in line for the Pipe crown, puts it succinctly: "What he does is poetry. For sheer beauty, no one else even comes close."

Surf historian Matt Warshaw puts it poetically: "Nobody cat-walked Pipeline before Gerry. He invented the whole ballet act. Lopez rode Pipe like Audrey Hepburn stepping out of a cab on 5th Ave."

The first surfer Gerry emulated was his hero Paul Strauch.

"When I first saw Paul surf, I really admired everything about him. He was the kind of surfer I wanted to be like." Paul Strauch, for the record, is one of four legendary surfers chosen personally by Duke Kahanamoku as heirs—to continue introducing the magic of surfing and the Aloha spirit throughout the world.

"There are a lot of great surfers from his generation—and mine too," Gerry continues. "But none of them had the elegance, style, and grace that Paul Strauch does."

"My father," he mentions next, "was very close with the beach boys of the early era. He was a master net fisherman, the equivalent of being a lariat expert in horse country. He taught me to surf. I think he gave me my patience."

Born on November 7, 1948, in Honolulu, Hawaii, Gerald Ken Lopez is of Japanese, German, and Spanish descent—the son of a high school teacher mother and newspaperman father.

"I started surfing when I was about nine at Waikiki," Gerry says, "but only really began to be serious about it when I was attending Punahou School."

Randy Rarick, cofounder of professional surfing (now the World Surf League) and a contemporary of Gerry's, recalls a funny story about Gerry when they all first started board riding.

"We lived in the same neighborhood and were friends," Randy remembers, "but my house was right at the beach and Gerry's family was up the hill. The

surf spot was in front of my house. The best rides peeled right, and a slower, friendlier wave peeled left. So when Gerry would come down to surf, the older kids would make him ride the left-hand peak." Randy laughs. "Later, when Gerry was the maestro of surfing lefts, we'd always joke that he became so good going left because he *had* to practice for years on the left-hander at our spot."

Competing as a teenager, he won the 1966 Hawaiian Junior Surfing Championships and was a finalist in the Hawaiian state titles in 1968 and 1969. His reputation was growing. His boards were being noticed, and he was shaping a few for money.

But a career as a competitive surfer can be short-lived and is often unsuccessful. And the pay was poor and sporadic—especially in the late 1960s, before the professional circuit was organized. Gerry needed stability—and direction. He was looking for inspiration, for focus. In retrospect, his rise to fame seems almost preordained. But the years on the tightrope before his ultimate recognition were no cakewalk.

Like almost everyone who becomes an iconic figure on the path they pursue, greatness is not assured—no matter how relentless their determination, what skills they are born with, or how hard they work. They also need luck. Greatness requires skills, determination, and hard work, but a bolt of lightning still needs to strike—often more than once. In Gerry's case, it could be said to have resembled an electrical storm.

## Life #4. Becoming Mr. Pipeline

Gerry's first lightning strike was his early association with Dick Brewer, the acknowledged guru of Hawaiian shaping. Very few significant changes in history can be traced to a single moment in time. But Maui was a fertile crossroads for the entire counterculture of the '60s, and in December 1967,

*Gerry Lopez in 1971 at Pipeline, Oahu, Hawaii. Photo by Jeff Divine*

a group of Australians visited the island to test their new shaping concepts at the fabled near-perfect right-hand break at Honolua Bay. The group included 1966 world champion Nat Young. It also included Australia's single most important shaper, Bob McTavish, who was experimenting with boards far shorter than had ever been ridden for the first two decades of modern surfing.

Gerry was there, of course—it has always been part of his mojo to turn up when cosmic spheres intersect. It was a seminal moment in surf history, when the world's two most influential shapers—Dick Brewer and Bob McTavish—met, exchanged ideas, and essentially set the stage for the short board revolution, the biggest change in the entire history of the sport.

"Brewer took the foam blank he had been promising to finish for me for weeks—and cut a foot off the nose!" Gerry recounts. "I jumped in, but he stopped me, saying, 'Lopez, I got this.' And then he takes his saw and cuts a foot off the *tail*! But when I rode the finished board, it worked like magic. And so did everyone else's."

Gerry took everything he observed from that meeting with the giants of shaping and began to develop his own designs that he felt fit his surfing. It was the first step in preparing for his debut on the world stage.

Not long afterward, he was offered a job shaping at Surf Line, Hawaii's leading surf shop of the era. His Waikiki surfing performances at Ala Moana reef were gaining notice. He and his friend and cohort Reno Abellira were both building a following as the hot new faces in Hawaii.

Surf Line was Gerry's second stroke of luck, for several reasons. It gave him a big boost in confidence and provided steady paying work. It was also where he honed his craft, developed design elements of his own, and began to make a name for himself as a shaper. Most importantly, though, he met a key life compatriot there: Jack Shipley, the shop manager. The two forged a bond almost immediately. From day one, they realized they complemented each

other as partners. Jack was gregarious, candid, funny, and outspoken. Gerry was reserved, serious, and dedicated to his craft. Gerry created the demand, while Jack handled the front end of the business.

"It was a snap to sell Gerry's boards," Jack remembers.

Then Gerry discovered yoga. His initial contact came almost serendipitously: "I saw these cute girls as I was passing a yoga class. I went there the next day hoping to find them again. One of them was heading the class, and as I watched, I thought: *Wow, it would be so great to be that limber, that in balance.*" He signed up and went to class.

"I loved it right from the very first day," he says. "I knew it would make me a better surfer. And that was what I knew I wanted to be."

But he became a complete devotee in 1969 when Swami Vishnudevananda Saraswati, founder of Sivananda Yoga, came to the University of Hawaii to lecture. Gerry infused his entire life focus with the techniques he was learning in this new transformative discipline. The practice interfaced with many aspects of the surfing lifestyle. It spoke to spirituality, health, and fitness; it centered his mind and gave him purpose—all things a young man in the turbulent 1960s was looking to find.

Later that same year, he headed to Huntington Beach for the US Surfing Championships, a highly publicized event with a huge crowd and lots of photographers. In the circus-like atmosphere, he found a quiet spot near the pier to sit. Closing his eyes, he assumed a full Lotus position to concentrate before his finals heat. Cameras flashed. He finished in fifth place, but this moment of meditative concentration became as noted as his surfing. Defining himself as one of the first surfers of his generation to shape his own equipment and also incorporate yoga into his life and career would have a leviathan influence. He was only twenty, but he had cemented two cornerstones of his psychic structure.

While both Gerry and Jack were thriving in the exploding growth of surfing at the end of the '60s, neither was content with the Surf Line owner's restrictive style.

"Gerry wanted to surf more and work less," Jack explains. "I wanted to market better and have more people like Gerry on the team."

"So one day," Gerry remembers, "Jack comes to me and says, 'Why don't we start our own shop?' And that was all it took. A few weeks later, we did."

Gerry and Jack went out on their own, renting the old Hobie shop on Kapiolani Boulevard, which had been the first retail surf shop in downtown Honolulu. A new life was beginning, but the fledgling partners had no inkling of what was about to happen—to them, to surfboards, to the surfing world itself. They had paddled for a wave that looked like it might be perfect. Now they were dropping straight down the face.

"We were on our way," Gerry says, smiling. "All we needed was a name!"

### *Life #5. Lightning Strikes Again*

At the Surf Museum's gala, dinner plates have been cleared, and the live auction has finished. Gerry's auction contribution, a striking red beauty with a bright golden pin line and logo accents, has gone for well over $10,000—a record for the event. The other guests of honor have received their awards. Honoree Fernando Aguerre roused the room with the announcement that his lifelong dream of bringing surfing to the Olympics had finally come true—surfing would be admitted to the 2020 games. Ever the belle of the ball, Jericho Poppler nearly stole the show with her Academy Award-like entrance to the stage after film star Gregory Harrison gave a "Best Actor in a Supporting Role" introduction for one of the true greats of women's surfing.

Nat Young, perhaps Australia's greatest surfer of his era, introduces Gerry, ending with a fiery accolade inviting him to accept his award and say a few words. The room comes to a standing ovation. Gerry rises from his chair and strolls toward the stage. Eight hundred eyes follow his step. Just as they had in those heady days of Lightning Bolt.

By the time he and Jack Shipley opened the modest little shop in 1970, the world around him had turned into a roller coaster ride. They had named the shop Lightning Bolt—a suggestion from Jack's wife.

"It was the logo that set us apart," Jack says.

In less than two years, Lightning Bolt surfboards vaulted into the most successful brand in the history of the sport. And so did Gerry. After missing the initial Pipeline Masters, he had won the event twice in a row, in 1972 and 1973. Now the undisputed reigning monarch at Pipeline, he was at the pinnacle of his prominence as a surf star. He'd been on a dozen magazine covers and anchored the critical sequences in nearly every surf film of the 1970s.

Around the globe, Bolt boards became so coveted that an entire stable of shapers was employed to fill the demand. In his own particular moment of marketing brilliance, Jack Shipley had given a Lightning Bolt surfboard to every top surfer on the North Shore, where half of the magazine shots came from each year.

"It was pure genius," remarks Gerry. "Now they weren't just shooting me at Pipeline; they were shooting every great surfer in Hawaii—riding *our* boards."

At one point, four future world champions were riding Bolts—*together in the same surf session.*

"We hardly needed to advertise." Jack laughs thinking back on it today. "We'd have twenty editorial pages of shots—with our logo showing—in every issue [of *SURFER* magazine]."

While Gerry credited his peak performances to his new, improved equipment, the world acclaimed the hero. When someone asked Waimea Bay surf legend Greg Noll if Gerry's success was due to his better boards, Da Bull answered, "No, it's his *bigger balls.*"

Hang Ten founder Duke Boyd approached the dynamic duo with an offer to take that little lightning bolt and do exactly what Hang Ten's two little feet had done: become a global phenomenon.

Jack and Gerry were elated. It seemed like a dream. Lightning Bolt products were flying out the door. The Bolt was attached to T-shirts, sunglasses, backpacks, bodyboards, towels, footwear, hats, jewelry…"just about anything," Jack recounts. "It transformed Lightning Bolt into a multinational corporation."

Gerry was able to travel to wherever he pleased. The checkbook was open. He pioneered Grajagan, the almost mythical Indonesian surf spot where the long hollow point broke like two dozen Pipelines in a row. By the end of the '70s, his life began to blur into a swirl of exotic travel, New York fashion models, Hollywood movie roles, and crazy parties. The cat was licking the rich cream from the bowl.

But all was not well in Bolt-land. Trouble started soon after the brand began to massively grow. There were four shareholders: Jack Shipley, Gerry Lopez, Duke Boyd's group, and the master licensee, Keepers Inc.

"We started out with 'A Pure Source' as our statement," recalls Jack. "And our surfboards *were*. But then the business exploded, the products proliferated, and the money started pouring in. Duke and Keepers started fighting about how the money was going to be spent."

Everyone had a different view.

"Duke and his group wanted to keep control of the logo," says Jack. "The licensee thought there was too much product out there and wanted more control. I thought we shouldn't hurt the brand reputation by making inferior products. Gerry just wanted to shape boards and go surfing."

Gerry sought guidance from Gordon "Grubby" Clark, whose foam blanks business had made him a giant of the surf industry. Grubby and other top surf moguls told Gerry the brand was in too much turmoil. They advised him to sell his shares and get out. Keepers, the licensee, was the only shareholder who was well-financed enough to buy Gerry's shares. Gerry's mentors had counseled him to get out before a crash. Gerry did. Jack didn't.

Did Gerry sell out? Did he take the money and run? I had heard of this saga years ago, but from only one side. So I asked Jack point-blank, "Did Gerry leave you in the lurch?"

"On the contrary," Jack declares. "He begged me to come with him. He took Grubby's advice. I took my own. He made the right choice." That was all there was to it. No collusion. No treachery. Just another good decision on the journey.

Not long after Gerry sold his shares, Lightning Bolt quietly folded. A thunderstorm is fast and furious, but it moves on very quickly. Gerry tried to make a go of an alternative brand, but the fire had gone out. The magic symbol that had set the world ablaze had become embroiled in a winner-take-all corporate battle that left it in ashes. But somehow Gerry had escaped—like a cat on a hot tin roof.

## *Life #6. Hollywood Does Surf*

At the gala, Gerry makes his way to the stage, weaving between the crowded tables. By the time he reaches the podium, the room is silent.

"Jesus," our emcee, Chris Cote, observes. "It's like he's a *movie star*."

"Well," I whisper, "he actually *is* a movie star."

It's not an idle claim. John Milius—the major motion picture director who wrote *Apocalypse Now*, *Jeremiah Johnson*, and *Magnum Force* as well as directing popular epics such as *The Wind and the Lion* and *Red Dawn*—gave him a call out of the blue to offer him a film role. Like almost every surfer who had grown up riding waves in the 1960s and '70s, Milius was a huge fan of Gerry's. The celebrated director brought Gerry in to play himself in *Big Wednesday*, Milius's magnum opus of Hollywood surf films. Milius gave Gerry costarring roles in *Conan the Barbarian* (as Arnold Schwarzenegger's sidekick) and *Farewell to the King* (as an island warrior fighting the Japanese). He also had roles in *North Shore* and *Baywatch*. He had been asked by a casting agent if he wanted to move to California permanently and start acting for a living.

One would think that a transition from sports star to film star would have been a natural career move. By the end of the 1980s, Gerry was no longer the hottest rising star in surfing's constellation. Lightning Bolt had had its day and was long gone. After a decade of media coverage, Grajagan was getting crowded. After five years of courtship, he had married his wife, Toni, in 1987, and had their son, Alex, in 1989. That same year, Gerry had starred in *Farewell to the King*.

But surprisingly, after looking at the commitment of time and energy and the constrictions on his first love—surfing—it would have required, Gerry declined a career on the silver screen. When his casting agent told him he would have to live full-time in Hollywood, Gerry replied, "You know what? I like Maui. I don't want to be an actor."

He left the film business and returned to the islands. Six lives lived. And still more to go.

## *Life #7. Attitude Dancing*

It was almost as if Gerry had shut the door on a particular era of his life. The 1990s would be a very different era. But those years would not be sedate. Gerry Lopez is not sedate. He is *serene*. One denotes a tranquilized state; the other, a calmness in the center of a storm.

He had already spent years learning to adapt his shaping to a variety of challenges. Now he would reinvent himself yet again, this time as a mentor to the next generation of surfers pushing the limits: the tow-in big-wave riders.

Gerry and his family had moved back to Maui. He and his brother, Victor (a longtime Maui resident), had viewed the giant outside reef at Peahi for years. And at a certain point, they came to consider it a rideable wave. Unbeknownst to them, the wave had been ridden in 1975, but then lain dormant after that. It was a sleeping giant if there ever was one. According to fellow surfer Darrick Doerner, "Gerry called us up one day and said, 'Hey, you guys gotta come over and check this thing out.' We did."

"We" in this case was a group of the best and most respected big-wave tow-in riders in the world: Laird Hamilton, Buzzy Kerbox, Dave Kalama, and Darrick Doerner himself. When the crew had a look at the place, they knew it was the ultimate mountain they wanted to ski down.

As their assault on this Everest of waves continued, they began to look for boards that would fit those waves best. Soon they were riding Gerry Lopez signature models. Once again Gerry had found a spot, analyzed the challenge, and developed a design element to conquer that challenge—and made it look

easy. He had even paddled out with them on a big day. Asked how he felt going out there for the first time, he replied with the quote attributed to Sioux warrior Crazy Horse before the battle of Little Big Horn: "Today is a good day to die."

Gerry did not die, however; in fact, another life was coming up. In 1988, he discovered snowboarding on a Mount Shasta Christmas trip his wife had coaxed him into. It began a love affair with the mountains. Then they began visiting Bend, Oregon. In the winter of 1992–1993, they decided to buy a home there with Grubby Clark. Or as Gerry puts it, "Our *wives* decided to buy a home."

He muses, "Snowboarding made me appreciate the surf even more than I did already. The ocean is always moving, always in flux. The mountains are solid, immovable. Snow and waves are two of the most unbelievable wonders of nature." As with other sports, Gerry became an expert snowboarder.

## Life #8. What You See

The gala is quiet now, the attendees listening to every word as Gerry speaks in his soft, precise manner. Even though it has been nearly forty minutes since Gerry started to talk, not a single person has left their seat even for a moment. The crowd remains patient. Even reverent. Gerry is paying homage now to all the people and things that have influenced his life. "Practicing yoga has enabled my surfing to stay at a level that would have been impossible without it," he notes. He talks about Duke Kahanamoku and Aloha Spirit, the Hawaiian spirit of generosity and welcomeness. He praises Rell Sunn who embodied that spirit. I recognize their connection even if Gerry does not. Like Gerry, Rell Sunn was never a world champion. She never even won a World Tour contest. But there is no woman in Hawaii—surfer or otherwise—who is more revered. Or who worked harder to make it all look easy.

Gerry's good friend George Kam has an insight that illuminates some of the reality behind the legend. "What many people don't see is the intense amount of effort that Gerry puts into everything he does. He's like Kobe Bryant. Nobody saw how hard Kobe practiced. They just saw him at game time."

George's observation is accurate. I remember watching *Five Summer Stories*, one of the seminal surf films of the 1970s. Gerry has a starring role and, in a dozen filmed rides, cemented his reputation.

"What the film doesn't show is the number of times Lopez *doesn't* make the wave—the times he wipes out, face-plants, gets pitched, and crashes hard," explains Randy Rarick, who watched the filming from the beach.

George agrees. "He probably took more beatings at Pipe than *anybody*," he notes. "Gerry used to say, 'You surf Pipeline, you better keep your wallet out. Because sooner or later, you are gonna have to pay.' And Gerry found out himself." Indeed. On a wipeout, he was flipped up in the air and landed butt-first on the fin of his upside-down board. The details are gruesome.

"He's just an incredible athlete," says his friend and mentor Grubby Clark. "Kitesurfing, stand-up paddling, snowboarding, windsurfing, foiling…. He's *really* good at them all. But what a lot of people don't know is he's an excellent motorcycle rider."

"It's probably true of a lot of exceptional people," notes Jack Shipley, "but he had an amazing set of parents. His mom and dad were great tennis players and both incredibly smart."

Here's an under-credited insight: "He's got stamina to burn," says Grubby Clark. "Most of us think of a surf session as one to three hours. Not Gerry—he can stay out for eight hours straight. So he gets the good waves sooner or later."

"Gerry doesn't really have a secret at all," says Grubby. "He's just a really nice, quiet, easygoing guy. He's the best guy in the world to take with you on a road trip. He's intelligent, he's very well read, he gets good advice and uses it. And he knows more about surfing than anyone anywhere."

"Gerry is a crafty guy," Jack Shipley chuckles. "He always came to the table from a different, really original place. He has a special psyche."

That brought up an accusation about Lopez the Pipe rider: how ruthless he was in taking waves. So many of my friends had remarked about that over the years, and I was aways somewhat shocked by the claim. Which is why in the recent biopic *The Yin and Yang of Gerry Lopez* (by skate wizard and film director Stacy Peralta), Gerry addresses the charge right off the bat.

"I just want to apologize to all the people I stole waves from," Gerry says in the opening lines of the movie. "I know my surfing is a subject of admiration." Then he admits, "The way my surfing got to that level was by stealing a lot of waves from other surfers."

He goes on: "And if you do it enough—and I did it a *lot*—you can become pretty good at it. You also stop thinking about *what a low thing it is*." What more can one do than to confess our sins and ask for forgiveness?

One thing Gerry *does* do is help people in a very simple but effective manner. And he does it in many ways, with many people. Peter "PT" Townend, the first World Surf League world champ, remembers how once, when PT was a young kid, Gerry was visiting for an event. PT asked Gerry for his advice.

"I told him I was having trouble making it out of the barrel," says PT.

GERRY LOPEZ | 49

"Let me tell you a little secret," Gerry confided. "You see that big water pipe over there? The next time you're in the tube and having trouble, take your front hand and point it straight at the center of the cylinder."

"I went back to Kirra the very next day," PT recalls, "and every time I put my hand in the eye of the cylinder, I started making it out of the tube." He laughs. "It was a simple tip, but I never forgot it."

Grubby Clark concurs: "My job making foam blanks was to provide the surfboard manufacturers with the right base material," Grubby explains. "When the shapes and sizes would change, I had to figure out what the main direction would be for shapers' needs. Gerry helped me out more than any other surfer in the industry."

The list of people Gerry has helped is long and varied. It includes me: when Gerry came to the Surf Museum's gala, it was their most successful event ever.

Gerry is ending his gala speech now, and his parting words are memorable—yet so simple: "No matter what else happens, no matter how old you are or how sad you are, or how tired you are—*keep paddling. Just keep paddling.*"

When it comes to Gerry Lopez, what you see is what you get. What appears to be a very enigmatic idol is really just a smart, talented, lucky, hard-working man with some seriously good instincts. And of course an aura that everyone recognizes but him.

Like Vermeer's magnificent painting technique, Michael Jordan's gravity-defying leaps, or Hemingway's spare prose, Gerry Lopez's wave dances were deceptively simple. But they were also astonishing in their effortless beauty.

"He was the perfect guy, with the best equipment at the perfect time, at the perfect place when it was the perfect opportunity," says Randy Rarick. "It was a rare moment."

"What is impressive is how Gerry continues to explore the world," says George Kam. "Big-wave adventure, traveling to special spots in Baja, teaching yoga classes, learning to foil…" George is on a roll now: "He's never afraid to try something new. He masters an artificial wave at the Surf Ranch. Or river waves at the Bend Whitewater Park in Oregon. Gerry surfs there almost every day.

"His zenith of achievement came a half century ago," concludes George. "Yet he may in many ways be more relevant today than he has ever been. He doesn't give up."

### Life #9. There is No Life Nine

Gerry has more lives to live. Maybe even nine more…

*Rell Sunn in 1980 at Makaha, Oahu, Hawaii. Photo by Jeff Divine*

# 3.

## RELL SUNN

### By Karen Rinaldi

*"As I write this, my back is supported by a hand-embroidered pillow made in honor of Rell, a serendipitous find at one of my local surf shops, Glide, in Asbury Park, New Jersey. I'd recently come off a pretty tough year of multiple surgeries and chemo treatments, and the pillow became a kind of talisman. In reading about Rell's own battle with cancer, I'd found the strength to return to the water even when I felt depleted. I found solace in the shared experience with this sister from another universe entirely, one I secretly coveted but in ways that weren't entirely concrete. I had my own very full life to live, but the call of a life devoted to time in the ocean would never cease whispering in my ear—a kind of tinnitus of longing. In any case, the pillow was a kitschy find that would literally have my back."*

PUBLISHER, EDITOR, AND AUTHOR KAREN RINALDI TELLS A VERY PERSONAL STORY about legendary Hawaiian surfer Rell Sunn whose diagnosis of breast cancer mirrored her own. An icon in women's surfing and a pioneer in women's health, Sunn cofounded the Women's International Surfing Association (WISA), which was the first women's pro circuit, and also had the distinction of becoming Hawaii's first female lifeguard. When Sunn was diagnosed with advanced breast cancer in 1982, she was given one year to live. She would outlive that prognosis by fifteen years, continuing to surf while establishing programs for breast cancer awareness, then a cultural topic of shame in Hawaii. Sunn became a beacon of hope for Karen in the face of her own diagnosis, with her goal to return to the water and surf again as Sunn had done.

# A HEART SHINING THROUGH DARKNESS

The sound of the *hohoa* as it lands repeatedly and quickly on the bark laid out over the wooden anvil makes a satisfying percussive music, in concert with the birds and the loud hum of a huge standing fan turned on high to keep us cool in the late-morning heat.

"You have to hold the beater lightly," Dalani explains as she taps. "You want to finesse the fibers to thin them and spread them out gently—you don't want to bang away with force and mangle it. That's what the guys do—they smash it like a club!"

I'm in Makaha on the Waianae coast of Oahu with my friend Grace Moon, visiting with Dalani Tanahy, a kapa artist, keeper of the Hawaiian tradition of making cloth from the bark of native trees, which Dalani shows us are growing all over her property. Even though we arrived well before noon, the hot and arid climate on this side of the island is inescapable. We sit under a large canopy, in what looks to be an open garage filled with tools and work surfaces, to shield us from the sun. As Dalani talks, she unceremoniously grabs a branch and begins scraping the outer bark with a sharp knife, nary a glance at her fast-working, expert hands.

We're in Makaha to talk story. Or, to be more accurate, to listen to Dalani talk story. Grace is writing a history of the Hawaiian Renaissance, and I am along for the ride, hoping to hear some firsthand stories about Rell Sunn for the homage to her that I'm writing for this book. This visit to the Waianae coast is a fortuitous gift Hawaii offered.

Dalani is tall and powerful. A stately woman in slippers and shorts, with a dark, unruly mane of hair. A woman clearly in command of her environment. She talks with a slight pidgin inflection, which this *haole* has come to find deliriously intoxicating. Language has held sway over my senses since I was a child, and Hawaiian pidgin has captivated me. The fullness of its sound and its cadence has a warmth mixed with wryness that welcomes but also reminds the visitor of their status as visitor.

Dalani hands over the beater and says, "Here, give it a try."

The hefty weight of the smooth and rounded, bulky wooden *hohoa* feels good in my hand, as if the tool itself commands the necessary movement for its intended effect.

I tap the bark to spread and push the fibers without tearing them. A hole appears, and I attempt to tap and roll to reconnect the fibers the way Dalani instructed a few moments earlier.

"Look, you're a natural!" Dalani generously offers with a big laugh, even though I am failing to get the desired effect to close the hole.

"This reminds me of spreading pizza dough!" I declare.

My New Jersey Italian roots assert themselves without a filter, and I go on the explain: "It's one of the simplest but most confounding things to do: to spread the dough evenly in a sheet pan without making holes in the dough!"

I realize what I'm saying has no relevance to either Dalani or Grace, so I stuff it and keep tapping. The burst let slip my brain's effort to make a connection between being here now with this majestic waterwoman in Makaha learning to make traditional kapa cloth, and my worlds-away Italian-American surfless upbringing in suburban northern New Jersey. My next thought was to wonder if I might have offended the ancestors and gods of these sacred lands by daring to compare making kapa to making pizza. I silently ask them for forgiveness.

I'm a latecomer to Hawaii, though not to her culture. Like most things in my life, I indulge my interest through voracious reading. As a publisher, editor, and writer, it's where I feel most comfortable—in the realm of books, words, language. At least that's where I landed in my late twenties after years of tug-of-war between living the life of the mind versus a more physical existence. What I couldn't grasp in my younger years was that separating a life of the mind from the life of the body was to bifurcate the self, so here I am in the middle of life's journey (I'm being generous with my personal timeline here) trying to reconcile that split.

In the ongoing discomfort I can sometimes feel about not having enough time in the ocean—more time, that is, with my embodied self—I torture myself about some of the decisions I've made along the way. Don't get me wrong; my life is mostly awesome and fulfilling. I've managed to have both surfing in my life and a career in publishing and as a writer. I'd be ungrateful to lob any complaints. But anyone who surfs will tell you that you have to choose to focus on one and put the other into the realm of sideline. I am, admittedly, greedy for the things I love. In the end, I chose to live in New York City and to devote my time to books. When the call of the ocean became too strong to ignore, I attempted to learn to surf late in life (many would say a fool's errand,

and they wouldn't be wrong), believing I'd try once, get it out of my system, and finally quell the siren call of the ocean.

That didn't work. Rather, it manifested this life of contradiction and tension. These last two decades have been a not-always-successful effort to have it both ways. The result: as a surfer, I will forever be a beginner. Still, I devote a good deal of time and resources to do something I will never be good at. As Grace says, "You're not as bad a surfer as you think you are." In that "as bad" lies truth: I suck at surfing. I even wrote a book about it to try to figure out why I persist. Alex Dick-Read, the former editor-in-chief of the wonderful but now defunct magazine *The Surfer's Path* asked me once when I was complaining about this tension: "So what would you rather be? A better publisher or a better surfer?"

I reflexively answered, "Publisher." But the question would haunt me. Still does.

Hawaii would have remained for me in the realm of mind, rather than body, had it not been for my friend Grace, who grew up in Honolulu. The circumstances of our relationship ultimately led to her insistence that I join her on an extended stay on the South Shore. As a kook and a *haole*, I was all too familiar with the ways in which I might fumble, and the thought of making a trip to Hawaii to surf seemed nothing less than absurd. For the past twenty-plus years, I'd surfed mostly in New Jersey and Costa Rica on beach breaks. The aqua blue reef breaks of Hawaii were for the more talented and deserving surfers—at least this is the story I'd told myself. And if I'm honest about it, I was just plain scared. Also, I'd read plenty about first contact, colonization; I've listened to the heartbreaking music that tells of the devastation brought about by the white man. I was conflicted even entertaining the idea. Traveling to Hawaii to surf as the kook that I am seemed an exercise of both entitlement and folly. Besides, the Hawaiian breaks didn't need me mucking up the lineup.

This is no false modesty, I assure you. So, Hawaii remained in the purview of my dreams. Until I met Grace.

Before I met Grace, I met Rell Sunn. Not in person, alas, but, maybe fittingly, in a story. I'd read *Fierce Heart: The Story of Makaha and the Soul of Hawaiian Surfing* by Stuart Holmes Coleman, and the *Surfer's Journal* piece "A Visit to Rell's Motel" by Mark Cunningham. Rell's motel-like home—where people were welcome day and night to come hang, borrow boards, surf, crash, eat—rang true to my own little house by the ocean. A friend once wrote on the back of my pantry door: "Your home is like a giant surfboard closet with food." That has a ring of heaven to it.

Still, in my life as a publisher and editor living mostly in New York City, I spent more time in words than water, so my stoke often came from story. My surf library is vast, and most of those books and articles and stories were from and about men. If you do a Google search for famous people from the Waianae coast, you'll find musician Israel Kamakawiwoʻole and actor Jason Momoa and two other dudes, but not Rell. So I sought out stories about women, and Rell's stayed with me. When a few years after I'd discovered Rell I was diagnosed with breast cancer, she became a beacon for me.

As I write this, my back is supported by a hand-embroidered pillow made in honor of Rell, a serendipitous find at one of my local surf shops, Glide, in Asbury Park, New Jersey. I'd recently come off a pretty tough year of multiple surgeries and chemo treatments, and the pillow became a kind of talisman. In reading about Rell's own battle with cancer, I'd found the strength to return to the water even when I felt depleted. I found solace in the shared experience with this sister from another universe entirely, one I secretly coveted but in ways that weren't entirely concrete. I had my own very full life to live, but the call of a life devoted to time in the ocean would never cease whispering in my ear—a kind of tinnitus of longing. In any case, the pillow was a kitschy find that would literally have my back.

    A once-vibrant but now sun-faded, much-loved-and-worn eighteen-inch-square poof, the pillow captures highlights of Rell's life and character familiar to all who knew her or who've read any story about her: In the center of the pillow is a beautiful embroidered portrait of Rell, with her long, flowing dark hair, a pink hibiscus tucked behind her right ear, a white lei adorning her neck. Underneath her portrait are the words "Heart of the Sea"—a translation of her Hawaiian name, Kapolioka'ehukai. Surrounding Rell are smaller embroidered images of her in all of her glory: as an expert free diver and spearfisher, hula dancer, world-class surfer, black belt, canoe paddler; and on a longboard with her moniker, "Queen of Makaha," crowning her head. Even her beloved dog, Shane, makes the pillow. In my favorite threaded image, Rell nose-rides a longboard along a bright blue head-high wave, with Shane riding in tandem as a rainbow surrounds them. The love and attention put into making this piece of pillow art speaks to the reverence and love Rell inspires. Kitschy? Yeah, maybe. But for all of surfing's cool demeanor, kitsch this earnest brings pure joy.

The high points of Rell's story can be found in any account of her life. Born in a Quonset hut in Makaha on July 31, 1950, she began to surf at the age of four. Nicknamed "Rella Propella" by her grandmother, Rell had energy to burn. From an early age, she lived her mantra that you mustn't fear the ocean but you must respect it—a mantra I struggle to maintain in my own life. My respect is matched by my fear, which does nothing to help me in the waves. I envy the influences in Rell's life—her beach-boy father; an uncle of no less stature than the surfer king of Makaha, "Buffalo" Keaulana; the very ocean herself; and a community whose lives centered on the sea. Rell felt protected by the gods and ancestors when she was in the ocean, convinced nothing bad would ever happen to her there. As Rell grew up, she quickly proved herself to be a fierce and talented waterwoman—as good a diver as she was a surfer. She traveled the world to surf, won contests, and became one of the first women's surf champions. Rell was also the first female lifeguard among the legendary Hawaiian lifeguards.

During one of the Makaha International Surfing Championships in the 1960s, Rell listened to all of the surfers talking story, and was inspired to become a voice for women in the surf world. As she says in the film documenting her life, *Heart of the Sea*, all she heard were "men telling great stories, and I said, 'Women could tell those stories, too!'" She made the decision then to create the stories she would tell.

This is a refrain surrounding Rell's legacy and the stories everyone tells about her, many of them about women and surfing. While historically, women surfed as much as men in Hawaii, women's place in the surfing world took a back seat after surfing went through its renaissance in the early twentieth century. Rell and a few of her friends would set out to change that.

Dalani told us how, years ago, she'd read only about men in the local *H3O* magazine—when there were plenty of women out there ripping. She approached the editor and said, "Hey, where are all the women?" *H3O*, so-called for "heavy water," was about riding big waves. Even though women were holding their own in big surf, until Dalani pushed the issue, no one thought to write about them. Dalani took the matter in hand.

Where there was no surf club for women, Rell and Dalani created the Westside Wahine Surf Club. While Rell was clearly generous to all, her instinct and tenacity to create space for women broke all kinds of barriers for women surfers. As Cambridge literature don and surfer Andy Martin wrote about her in an obituary for *The Guardian*: "She harked back to an ancient Hawaiian tradition, exemplified by such semi-legendary figures as Hina'ikamalama and Kele'a who, in the era before European contact, were reputed to be better surfers than men. When Captain Cook sailed into the islands for the first time, he noticed that men and women were equally adept in the field of water sports. The 19th-century evangelists soon put a stop to all such pagan pursuits. It was Sunn who put women back in the water."

Rell shone like her surname, and her legacy of bringing aloha to all she did has been reported in every account of her life story. Andy Martin quoted Brian Keaulana, a fellow lifeguard, who said of her, "Rell was the greatest in surfing, swimming, sailing, spearfishing—but more than that, she was the embodiment of the aloha spirit."

My proximity to Rell could never get closer than one degree of separation—but I thrilled even to that one degree. On a previous trip to Oahu, I met Luana Froiseth, another of the great Hawaiian waterwomen. I'd read all about Luana's father, Wally Froiseth, in my meanderings through every bit of surf literature I could get my hands on. Froiseth *père* was a surf pioneer and legend, but Luana was unknown to me until Grace introduced us. (Stories of waterwomen are still woefully absent from much of the surf histories.) Luana, at sixty-nine, is mighty in both presence and story. She was a professional surfer and champion canoe paddler, is currently president of the Waikiki Surf Club, and has been a leader in the Outrigger Canoe Federation.

Luana knew Rell and her family and tells of how, when they were just kids, Rell and her sisters snatched Luana's surfboard from the beach and paddled out. Rell's family couldn't afford surfboards, so she and her sisters had to be resourceful, even if it meant "borrowing" someone else's board. Luana said she just waited patiently on the beach until Rell returned the board when she was done. Luana recounts the story with a knowing smile, a nod, and a look into the distance as if to say something more, but I don't push. I don't feel I have the right to. But in her animating way of talking story, Luana seems to project an intimate image from her mind that helps me to picture Rell as that feisty little girl her grandmother called Rella Propella.

I was visiting Luana at her house in the hills above Diamond Head by the grace of Grace—who had become a kind of surf angel for me. My life had recently fallen apart, and my access to surfing had become much more difficult. I'd previously worked hard to arrange my life to ease this friction between surfing and work. And while I still hadn't been able to get in the water as much as I wanted to, I had a house in proximity to the ocean, so I could usually squeeze in a session if there were waves. I lost that home, and my access to waves has become more tenuous. Grace appeared in my life like the blessing she is in many ways, not the least of which is her insistence that I do whatever I have to do to get in the water.

Grace and I had met a few years before she invited me to visit Luana with her, and our friendship has become one of those late-in-life connections that feels fated. When I saw her walk into a book reading—we were at Pilgrim Surf + Supply in Williamsburg, Brooklyn—I spotted her and thought: *I want to know that woman.* The surf bond was immediate by virtue of where we were—the surf community in New York City is small but tenacious. We talked and were immediately at ease with one another. She was writing a book on Hawaii; I was interested for both personal and professional reasons; she needed advice on writing and publishing. We kept in touch sporadically, but it wasn't until she called me to seek advice of a different kind that we forged a deeper bond. Grace had just been diagnosed with breast cancer.

Throughout her life, Rell was all about this bond of women helping other women in spaces where help didn't exist. She was true to the tradition of creating women's circles. An important part of her legacy was bringing awareness about cancer screenings to Hawaii. Until Rell, a reluctance for women to openly share experiences about illness created a harmful reticence—especially concerning so-called women's illnesses. Women would get sick and die of breast cancer in silence from the dearth of readily available information and updated standards of care. Rell made use of her own diagnosis and experience to gather women together to help shed the shame and the implicit cultural discretion preventing women from talking about their own bodies. In doing so, she moved the needle further toward helping women to learn protocols for self-examination and to understand the importance of screening for early detection. She wasn't only a pioneer in surfing; she was one in women's health as well.

I don't know what I would have done when I was diagnosed with breast cancer if I hadn't been able to tap into a community of women who had also been through it. In those connections, I found support, information, and not least important, gallows humor. I'll never forget the tenor of my first conversation with Grace about breast cancer. Somehow, we laughed a lot. I don't recall the details, except her asking my advice about reconstruction (I have a lot to say about it, but this isn't the space to delve into it…), but mostly I was struck by how, through these major life setbacks, we were able to find humor in the darkness. Rell had found it too. A friend of hers discovered a prosthesis for Rell to use after her mastectomy, which she sewed into her bathing suit. Rell called that friend her "bosom buddy." When the prosthesis came undone during a surf session, she combed the beach looking for it. When someone asked her, "Aunty Rell, what are you looking for?" she said, "My boob!"

*Rell Sunn in 1981 in Taapuna, Tahiti. Photo by Jeff Divine*

Cancer didn't slow Rell down. When she was released from MD Anderson Cancer Center in Houston, Texas, after an intense treatment that put her into a coma from which she nearly didn't awake, she returned to Makaha to help organize the first all-women's surf meet. Rell tells about the visions she kept having when she was in the coma. She kept paddling for waves, but she couldn't catch them. She'd paddle and miss, paddle and miss. (Interestingly, she doesn't blame herself for these misses; she says the waves weren't breaking or strong enough to catch. I mention this here as an indication of the power of perspective—another lesson from Rell.) Finally, a nice wave came and she paddled for it; it crested, and she caught the wave. She awoke from her coma right at that moment and said to her sister, who was sitting at her bedside, "Did you see that? I finally caught a wave!" Her sister thought they were going to lose her. Rell swears that surfing saved her life.

Shortly thereafter, back in Hawaii at the surf contest, Rell signed up for every event. She was thin and worn from treatment, but sure enough, she won the title. Rell was not a person to wallow in self-pity—though I'm sure I'm not alone in thinking that surfing can be a hell of an incentive to not die.

When I was diagnosed, my first thought was, *Will I get to see my children grow up?* My second was, *Will I get to surf again?* (It wasn't, it must be said, *Will I get to publish another book?*) Getting back in the water after each surgery was paramount. My surgeons and oncologists, as Rell's did, seemed to take the surfing remedy seriously. Not once did they tell me I couldn't surf. They provided me with waterproof bandages when necessary and told me what kind of sports bra to wear. Only once, a physical therapist recommended that I put off surfing due to some cording that had developed along the underside of my left arm, making it impossible for me to fully stretch it out and excruciating to even try.

I asked her, "What're my other options?"

She told me there wasn't one. I was not to surf.

I was heading to Costa Rica the following day, and I told her, "I am going to surf, so please help me find a solution."

Her response: "What is it with you surfers? You're all obsessed." She should have met Rell.

What became clear to me from my conversations with Luana and Dalani was a largely unacknowledged dark side of the Sunn. Dalani told us how she wrote about that in an *H3O* piece titled "The Dark Side of the Sunn." I felt a surprised relief. As of this writing, I could not find a copy of the issue containing Dalani's story, but long after this has gone to print, I will keep searching for it. And even though I haven't read it, life has taught me that no one can shine that brightly without a corresponding shadow. For all of the celebration and inspiration Rell evokes, I admit that the unbidden mention of Dalani's piece captivated me and evoked a kind of giddiness. Rell's beauty and energy and goodness shone like the star of her name, but I welcomed hearing of a shadow side, partly because it was hidden, but more so because it makes my own less forbidding.

Looking for points of connection to this spirit sister I would never meet—at least not in this earthly lifetime—I found them most comfortingly in the darker sides of Rell's experience. Cancer would seem the most obvious. When she was diagnosed at the relatively young age of thirty-three and given one year to live, Rella Propella was having none of that. She had work to do and waves to catch. Her refusal to surrender gave her fourteen years of living with all the gusto of a grom while changing the lives of those she touched along the way. Perhaps most importantly, she got to see her daughter, Jan, grow up.

But cancer, for both of us, it seems, was not the nadir. While speaking with Dalani and Luana, Rell's romantic relationships seemed to invite some deeper examining if one were to understand more about Rell's life. The details are not important for my story here, but what I came to understand was how Rell's light was a beacon for all, including some who might cause her heartache. Rell had been married three times, as have I. This is no Zsa Zsa Gabor joke (do I date myself?) or braggadocio on my part but rather speaks of my lack of ability to find a good match for a partner. It would seem Rell suffered from a similar handicap. In my case, one marriage nearly killed me and another threatened my life in ways I should have foreseen but that I refused to acknowledge. There is a kind of delusion in this refusal and a stubborn denial about the shadowed corners of my life that I've tried to avoid. Light is so much more fun! Like everything, there is never one without the other. Every wisdom tradition tells us so.

Even though my search for Dalani's piece on Rell has come up short, the hints I've found about the pain points in Rell's life are spare, but pointed, and involve both conjecture and instinct on my part. For example, on reading Greg Ambrose's oral biography *Stories of Rell Sunn: Queen of Makaha*—surprisingly the only published biography I could find on her—I felt closer to Rell by what went unsaid or by what fell between the lines. As an editor of several decades, I am trained to look for what is not said on the page, which often tells more or at least something different from what is said. My job, as I see it, is to help a writer tell the story she intends to tell to the extent that she can tell it. After working with hundreds of authors, you develop an ear for subtext and can decide how hard to push to bring that subtext above its burial. It's an instinct we all have as storytellers: to use and/or omit words, and to leverage our chosen language and stories to protect ourselves, others; to hide from ourselves, others; to lie to ourselves, others. In the stories not told about Rell and in the restraint of the oral biographic anecdotes—that was where I felt that the gold ore of Rell was hiding. But how to mine it? Especially when it wasn't mine to mine at all.

The mining to be done was into depths of my own shadows—which were proving to be slippery and abyssal. Living in the aftermath of having lost much of my hard-won security (all those years working as a publisher and not prioritizing surfing—much of it gone!), I struggled to reconcile the loss with the freedom necessary to my overall health and well-being. I knew the calculus was in my favor—I didn't have a choice to keep living as I had been—but I longed for stories I could learn from Rell. She'd helped me through cancer; could she also help me through the heartbreak of having betrayed oneself for another?

Still, the crux of this exegesis, about Rell and my connection to her via surfing—this very heart of the matter of surfing and how ineffable it is—has not been compromised by the dissolution of my last relationship, even as it has threatened my life in the ocean more than the cancer that threatened to kill me. I found some solace when I reread the *Surfer's Journal* piece.

In the story, Rell is careful (ever graceful) but clear about how people can hurt us so much more than illness. She acknowledges the loving support she received from Ann Cummings, in whose house she lived for most of her life. Rell explains, "She has seen me raise my daughter and go through two divorces and a devastating breakup in a relationship that set me back more than cancer did, emotionally and physically. It's a terrible thing to find disappointment in life." Here, in a moment of declared gratitude, Rell gives us a glimpse of truth through occlusion. Clearly, she had experienced, and shared with a friend, something traumatic in relation to someone she'd trusted, and that, I know viscerally, is the worst kind of pain.

But through it all, the more important part of this story, is how Ann was a beacon in her life in spite of the pain Rell suffered, which is how I've felt about

Rell for mine. It would seem on the surface that I have no life at all connected to Rell's, and yet that connection burns brightly across time, across oceans, across specific experiences.

When I think of Rell, when I hear and read and watch all of the stories about her, when I see the style and grace with which she danced on waves and witness her intrepid oceangoing life, all of her lightness, her big heart and status as queen, all of it lands so much more deeply when I also consider a corresponding shadow side. It's what makes her so alive to me. And that aliveness is a result of the dance between joy and sorrow: joy and sorrow are connectors.

Here's the beauty about connection—it transcends boundaries and sometimes it travels in one direction, in the same way unconditional love does. Love flows downriver, like the pull of gravity or the fierce pull of the heart, and moves inexorably toward the sea—or, we might say here, toward the heart of the sea. Only with obstruction will it eddy and swirl against the flow, against its first nature. So it is with water as it is with love. And connection—in all of its joy and sorrow—is love.

Rell will never know how her story is a palimpsest of my own, a story that keeps getting rewritten over and over again—for women, for surfers, for mothers, for survivors, and for those of us who eventually succumb—everywhere. It will get rewritten when I am also long gone: a story—or all stories—about the spirit that prevails through it all, about community and love.

If surfing, if indeed everything, isn't about love, then what is anything for? Rell embodied—even through the darkness, or maybe more so *because* of the darkness—a love that shone through everything, one that burned brightly and lasted. It always brought her back to the sea. Even at her low points, Rell would think about what it was she had to give. I write "think," but that is further conjecture on my part. Her actions divulged her giving heart. The thinking came in the planning for her doing. Toward the end of her life, having suffered through rounds of radiation and chemotherapy and relapses and metastases, she still managed to organize and accompany twenty youngsters to a surf contest in Biarritz, France. Another of her legacies, the Menehune Surf Contest in Makaha (in its forty-fifth year as of this writing) is yet another example of Rell's love flowing downriver, toward the sea, in an act of pure giving.

Rell's death in the early days of 1998 didn't extinguish her light. That light only shines brighter with every story told and received about her. It all comes back to story. It's what makes us human. At its best, it's what connects us—talking story. Surfers rely on it. Hawaiians make a life of it. Maybe we all do. We just have to hope that the stories we get to tell are more of generosity and kindness and love than they are of power-taking, grandiosity, and exclusion.

Sometimes, if we take a breath deep enough to connect New Jersey and Makaha, to connect my Italian heritage to Rell's Hawaiian one, my clumsy wipeouts to Rell's graceful gliding, Dalani and Luana's generosity to share time and story with me and Grace to Rell's and Grace's and my dance with breast cancer, and yes, to making pizza and making kapa, if we can hold in that one breath and in it capture and hold what unites us, we can then let go of the breath that contains the shadows threatening to keep us separate and alone. Darkness lives alongside the light, absolutely, but it doesn't have to hide it, in life or in death.

# 4.

## LAIRD HAMILTON

### By Sam George

*"What I was looking at, what we were all looking at—
and very soon the entire world would be looking at—
was nothing less than the most incredible wave anyone had ever
seen with a surfer on it: a backless, thirty-foot-high horizontal
hurricane, churning its way down the reef at Teahupoo
with a cylindrical eye that would swallow a high-rise."*

LAIRD HAMILTON IS CONSIDERED THE GREATEST BIG-WAVE SURFER of all time. A death-defying drop into Tahiti's behemoth of a wave, Teahupoo, on August 17, 2000, catapulted his status to mythic proportions when he emerged out of the enormous tunnel vortex in what was called the Millennium Wave. A photograph ran on the cover of *SURFER* magazine with the caption "oh my god…"

Former professional surfer, author, and director Sam George was the editor of *SURFER* magazine at the time. Here he shares the behind-the-scenes events that led up to and occurred on that day—an unexpected convergence of happenings that put Laird Hamilton on that wave at that time.

# LAIRD'S WAVE

It's one of the greatest surf stories never told. Or, to put it more accurately, the missing part of one of surfing's greatest stories. Missing, that is, until now.

It was the third week of August in 2000, and I arrived at the Capistrano Beach offices of *SURFER* magazine at my usual time. It was a warm, bright morning, early summer's "June gloom" long forgotten, and the pleasant, seven-mile bike ride up the Pacific Coast Highway from my home in San Clemente gave me ample time to review the day's editorial tasks awaiting my attention. Editor-in-chief of a surfing magazine might not have seemed like a "real" job to those whom legendary '60s surfer Phil Edwards characterized as "the legion of the unjazzed" (meaning non-surfers), but I and *SURFER*'s dedicated young staff took our positions as seriously as one might, while being able to show up for work with sandy feet in flip-flops. Yet something about this particular morning was different; an unexpected riffle of wind on an otherwise glassy swell. I felt it as soon as I walked in the door and saw the magazine's associate editor, photo editor, art director, and even publisher standing together in postures of contained expectation, as if they'd all been waiting for me to arrive.

"We got McKenna's photos from Tahiti," said someone (just who I honestly don't remember). But I knew exactly what they were talking about.

Seven days earlier, I'd been paid a visit by the already world-famous surfer Laird Hamilton. This in itself was an unusual occurrence—ordinarily you'd be expected to request, through channels, an audience with Laird if you wanted any one-on-one with him. I'd known Laird for over a decade, however, traveled with him on occasion, and throughout the years had, in the pages of *SURFER*, provided plenty of informed perspectives on his many exploits. Can't say we were friends, exactly, but I was pretty sure that Laird knew I got him. Which is probably why, on that August morning, he'd made the extraordinary exception of dropping by to give me a heads-up on a new exploit he had planned for later in the week. Either this, or he'd just wanted to see my reaction—the look on my face—when he told me that he was flying to Tahiti to confront a massive Southern Hemisphere swell, with plans to tow-in surf the fearsome tubes of Teahupoo.

Keep in mind that at this point in time Laird Hamilton was indisputably the best big-wave surfer the world had ever seen—having, as the primary driver of jet ski–powered tow-in surfing, spearheaded the sport's most significant paradigm-shifting, quantum-leaping innovation since 1935, when proto-designer Tom Blake first tacked a skeg to the bottom of his finless wooden plank. Even so, the tow-in surfing movement—which since 1993 had seen suitably motivated surfers riding tiny, high-performance surfboards being whipped into massive, previously unapproachable waves at the end of a ski rope—was being practiced at a select few offshore, deep-water breaks: Peahi, or "Jaws," on Maui, and Mavericks in Northern California being two prime examples. Scary, yes; dangerous, certainly, especially on those rare days when towing in seemed the only option: forty-, fifty-, even sixty-foot wave faces. Yet the challenge inherent in riding these sorts of waves, while magnified, was at least familiar to any surfer who'd cut their teeth in traditional big-wave arenas like Oahu's Waimea Bay or Sunset Beach. The trauma associated with being held down underwater following a tremendous wipeout was a well-known component of big-wave surfing, and the repeated survival of it tended to instill in the sport's heavy-water heroes what might be seen by some as remarkable confidence, and by others as sheer recklessness.

Nobody ever imagined, however, that anyone would attempt to tow-in to treacherously abrupt, shallow-water, razor-sharp coral reef break waves like those encountered at Teahupoo, on the main island of Tahiti in French Polynesia. For one thing, the use of foot straps—as is required in tow-in surfing—was seen as a potential death sentence at a break like Teahupoo, where surfers can be seen diving and even leaping away from their boards to avoid a fiberglass axe chop while caught in the vortex; being crushed against the shallow coral reef represented peril enough.

In addition, one of tow-in surfing's great advantages is that it allows the surfer standing at the end of the rope to be brought up to speed gradually, carefully matching the velocity of a massive, unbroken swell before it steepens to break, thus eliminating the last-second "elevator drop" that prone surfers must contend with. This advantage would be nullified at a spot like Teahupoo, where powerful Southern Hemisphere swells emerge almost undetected from the deep ocean and slam against a reef system that lies only a single fathom below the surface; literally rear up out of the depths with the weight of the entire Pacific at its back, then pour over with a curl of incomprehensible ferocity, daring surfers to confront its terrible concavity. Because of dramatically problematic aspects like these, conventional surfing wisdom had asserted that tow-in surfing at Teahupoo was impossible.

Which is precisely why it came as no surprise to me that Laird Hamilton was intent on proving the collective wrong.

"I've watched all the footage of those guys surfing Teahupoo," Laird told me that morning—"those guys," of course, referring to only the world's best surfers. "They're all taking off on the shoulder. I think that wave can be surfed further up the reef, from a way more critical takeoff spot."

Counting myself among those who felt that tow-surfing Teahupoo was sheer lunacy, I felt compelled to express some concern.

"But what if you blow the drop that far back, or if the barrel just runs past you?" I asked. "I mean, how do you survive a wipeout further up the reef, when those near the deep-water channel are bad enough?"

"Flotation," he said, matter-of-factly. "I'm going to wear a lightweight flotation vest."

"F-flotation?" I stammered, having never before heard of any surfer even considering the use of flotation in big waves. "Really? You sure you'd want to be at the surface when that second wave of the set hits you? How would you get under it?"

"That's not the point," Laird said. "I'm not worried about getting under the next wave. The vest is so that if I do go down on the kind of wave I'm looking for, my body will float up and give my rescue team enough time to reach me and start CPR."

OK.

"You know, Laird," I said, "a number of things run through my mind before I go surfing. Things I've got to think about, like wind, tide, what board to ride. I got to tell you, preparing for CPR isn't one of them. But good luck, man. And send photos."

Now, standing there at a light table in the *SURFER* magazine office, only a week after the conversation noted above took place, I was about to see the photos that Laird had sent me, fresh from the lab. Magnifying photo loupe in hand, I bent over a slide sheet of transparencies, but before I could begin a methodical review, photo editor Jason Murray stilled my hand.

"Just look at this one," he said, smiling as he indicated a particular slide several rows down on the plastic sheet. I placed the loupe on the sheet, leaned in, and focused on the tiny image.

"Oh my god," was all I could say.

According to ancient Greek mythology, it was the Oracle of Delphi who assigned the mighty Herakles (Hercules, in the Roman myth version) the "Twelve Labors," set down in order of difficulty, as a manner in which the hero might atone for previous sins. While surfing mythology has no Herakles, it does have Laird Hamilton, the next best thing. The major difference is that, unlike in the case of the half-blooded son of Zeus, Laird—whose name in Scottish means "lord"—assigned a consequential series of "labors" to himself; nobody tasked him with slaying the Nemean Lion, for example, or scourging the Augean Stables, taming the wild Mares of Diomedes, or capturing Cerberus, the three-headed guard dog of the Underworld. Then again, neither did anyone task Laird with moving from his bucolic home on Kauai to Oahu's hectic North Shore in the mid-1980s and immediately becoming a dominant force at the Banzai Pipeline, the world's most combative surf spot. Or applying himself to performing high-amplitude aerial flips at Backdoor Pipe wearing Velcro attachments on his feet. Or, on a twelve-foot paddleboard, bare-handing his way across the English Channel, the hard way, from Calais to Dover, then from the coast of Corsica to the isle of Elba. Or setting a European sailboarding speed record, ripping across the Netherlands' blustery coastal salt ponds at an unheard-of thirty-six knots. Or completely redefining big-wave surfing, creating mind-boggling new parameters of performance in the sport's most strenuous theater. Or almost single-handedly inventing stand-up paddleboarding, the world's fastest-growing watersport, or foil-surfing, the first entirely new way to ride waves in over five hundred years, or…or becoming quite simply the greatest ocean athlete the world has ever seen.

Strange, then, that unlike Herakles, who as a result of his exploits found himself worshipped in life as a demigod and then celebrated throughout the centuries with myriad stories, songs, and shrines, Laird—who, at a chiseled six-foot-three, 220 pounds, bears an uncanny resemblance to the ancient hero's many statues—had, by the end of the twentieth century, found himself an outlier in the remarkably conservative sphere of surfing celebrity. Vastly more talented, and in so many more ocean disciplines, Laird dwarfed the period's more conventional surf stars—both literally and figuratively. Deliberate or not (and it most probably was), Laird's relentless string of ocean exploits seemed to make a mockery of his fellow surfing heroes' seemingly one-dimensional surfing skills. A state of existence that, not surprisingly, earned him virtually no support from the established surfing industry. This was especially evident in certain quarters of the surf media. Case in point: when a particular editor at *Surfing* magazine, one of the sport's two most influential surf publications, vowed that no photo of Laird Hamilton would ever appear in the magazine's pages, despite the fact that Laird was at the time unquestionably the sport's greatest big-wave rider.

If this sort of dismissal bothered Laird, it was hard to tell. If so, the fact that in November 1998 he was featured on the cover of *National Geographic* magazine, a publication whose global circulation of six and a half million per month far outstripped *Surfing*'s eighty thousand or so, must have certainly tempered the sting. Nevertheless, not only did Laird not react to these blatant snubs from within, but he continued to do nothing to court the mainstream surfing media, only furthering his estrangement from the community he lorded over. Which is why, while many of his peers might have called Laird the very best, very few called him a friend.

To be fair, some of this aversion was earned, and even fostered, by Laird himself. Brash to the point of haughtiness, unflinchingly opinionated, fiercely demanding of subordinates and equally dismissive of lesser mortals, Laird was not always easy to be around. Quoted in an entry in historian Matt Warshaw's *Encyclopedia of Surfing*, '60s surfing legend Bill Hamilton described his stepson to be, at times, "mean…and gnarly."

A good portion of this reputation stems from Laird's deliberately cultivated "alpha male" persona. Though it would have been potentially a much more lucrative path, he saw no place for himself on any long-established surfwear company's roster of team riders; a relatively unknown German outdoor wear brand, whose imagery of Laird would go on to dominate its marketing efforts, suited him much better. Nor would sanctioned competition be the benchmark by which he'd be judged: not only did Laird have no respect for competitive surfing's established performance criteria, but to compete presented the possibility of falling short of someone else's standard. Laird's standard of performance, much like his many watery "labors," would be self-imposed or not at all. Small wonder, then, that a broad cross-section of surfing insiders (and more than a few outsiders) viewed Laird, though undeniably talented, to be the most irritatingly self-centered surfer to ever wax a board.

Then there was Lance Burkhart. Or rather, the character of Lance Burkhart, as portrayed in Universal Pictures' 1987 feature film *North Shore*, conceived and cowritten by producer Randal Kleiser (*Grease*, *The Blue Lagoon*). The film's plot centers around the travails of a young surf champion from Arizona (yes, there were wave pools, even back then) who makes his first pilgrimage to Oahu's fabled North Shore. There the hapless neophyte quickly finds himself at odds not only with fiercely territorial island surfers but fellow Pipeline Masters competitor Lance Burkhart, written as one of the most arrogant, stuck-up, and, by the film's climatic end, unscrupulous surf stars that any Hollywood screenwriter could possibly imagine. Played, inexplicably, by Laird Hamilton.

While many of the other well-known surfers featured in *North Shore* (Australians Robbie Page and Mark Occhilupo most notably) participated as if in on a grand joke, Laird appeared dead serious about inhabiting his role as the film's villain. Despite wooden delivery of the often excruciating dialogue (*"Chandler, you have a single-fin mentality. I need a bigger board with a lot more rocker"*), Laird's acting debut was spectacularly successful in merging the character of Lance Burkhart with his own, so much so that most viewers went away believing that, like the film's wise-cracking Aussies, he was simply playing himself—a perception that only hardened as time passed.

"Years later, I was in the shower at Ho'okipa [Beach Park]," Laird told me when I interviewed him about his *North Shore* experience for my 2010 feature documentary film *Hollywood Don't Surf*. "And this kid goes, 'Eh, you dat guy in dat movie, yeah?' And I'm like, 'But that's not me. I'm Laird, and that was Lance, a different person.' The little kid's like, 'Yeah, yeah,' and he sticks his hand out. So I go to put my hand out, and he pulls his hand away, saying, 'Brah, I don't shake hands with cheaters.'"

Laird smiled as he recounted that incident, but then again it was 2010, and by this stage in his life he could afford at least a small measure of self-deprecation. In August 2000, however, Laird was an entirely different animal, still dedicated at an almost metabolic level to triumphing over what he perceived as greater challenges and lesser men. Which is why, standing there at the *SURFER* magazine light table looking down at photographer Tim McKenna's perfectly framed shot from Teahupoo, all I could say was, "Oh my god."

*Laird Hamilton in 2023 in Malibu, California. Photo by Anne Menke*

What I was looking at, what we were all looking at—and very soon the entire world would be looking at—was nothing less than the most incredible wave anyone had ever seen with a surfer on it: a backless, thirty-foot-high horizontal hurricane, churning its way down the reef at Teahupoo with a cylindrical eye that would swallow a high-rise.

Not just that but, if it were real and not some Photoshop trick, it had to be the most mind-blowing, reality-altering, shake-your-head-to-make-sure-you-weren't-seeing-things, right-on-the-edge-of-unbelievable ride in surfing history: Laird tucked low and way back in the impossible curl, actually tracking below sea level as the monster wave's awesome hydraulics sucked water off the shallow coral shelf, being forced to strain with all his might against his tow board's foot straps, at the same time dragging his right arm in the wave face alongside the board, all in the supreme effort of maintaining his line and not being sucked up and over the falls into oblivion. Quite literally, and without any exaggeration, a do-or-die attempt on a wave the likes of which had never been seen before.

Of course Laird made it, as sequential photos and soon-to-be-released 16mm footage of the ride would show him successfully negotiating his way through the maelstrom, emerging triumphant from behind a blinding veil of exploding spray and sea mist, then gliding over the mutant wave's broad back before it expired onto the dry inside reef—Herakles vanquishing the Kraken. Of course we ran that first amazing McKenna shot on *SURFER*'s very next cover, along with the simple headline, "oh my god…," and it quickly became the bestselling newsstand issue in the magazine's forty-year history. Of course the imagery and stories of the epic ride went viral, swamping the internet before YouTube had even been invented, and of course (and as if the *National Geographic* cover hadn't been enough), the subsequent global coverage firmly established Laird Hamilton as the most famous surfer on the planet.

All of this without the world—surfing or otherwise—having any idea how truly remarkable that wave was, or how truly it reflected the nature of the man who rode it.

Thanks, Lance Burkhart. Because not even the dramatic cinematic account of Laird's Teahupoo plus ultra wave in director Stacy Peralta's fine 2004 documentary *Riding Giants*—in which Laird is depicted being moved to tears in the immediate aftermath, later admitting that the experience "softened some hard corners in my life"—actually moved the needle by much. In fact, what was now being called the "Millennium Wave" became regarded by many to be just another example of "Laird being Laird," one-upping his contemporaries with yet another outrageous feat, demanding our attention, daring the rest of the surfing community to question his rightful place at the sharp end of the spear. But as it turned out, those who thought this were wrong. Oh, it was Laird being Laird, alright, just not in the manner most people assumed—as I learned when I eventually heard the entire sequence of events that had led up to his epic ride.

Several weeks after the momentous Teahupoo session, I was talking with one of the other surfers who'd been there to witness the spectacle.

"It wasn't just that one wave," he said, "but the whole crazy day."

"Crazy how?" I asked. "You mean crazy big?"

"Just crazy," he said. "Like, with everything else that was going on, the whole session started out with Laird helping some guy who locked his keys in his car."

I had to tease the story out of Laird when I eventually got the chance to debrief with the man himself. Apparently, after spending a sleepless night listening to the biggest swell in living memory detonating on Tahiti's fringing barrier reefs, Laird and his entire team—which had included fellow big-wave hellman Darrick Doerner, legendary Tahitian surfer Vetea David, cinematographer Jack McCoy and his film crew, photographer Tim McKenna, associated assistants, acolytes, and a veritable fleet of personal watercraft—made their way along the island's flooded coastal highway to the end of the road, to the staging area in the village of Teahupoo. The size of the surf on the distant reef was difficult to comprehend, so beyond any previously known scale did it appear from shore. In other words: perfect for what Laird had in mind.

A frantic prep began: organizing camera equipment; tuning up surfboards, jet skis, and safety equipment; loading crew boats; with one eye on the massive swells booming like cannon fire offshore, and the other on the business of adequately preparing the numerous components associated with this first-ever attempt to tow-surf giant Teahupoo. Trying to stay calm, control the breathing, and free themselves from expectations about the outcome. Which was, of course, impossible. Who knew what the conditions were actually like out there, or how long they'd last? No one could predict the vagaries of swell size and direction, wind and tide; a surfer could be floating in the channel waiting for hours, or miss the peak of the swell by minutes. Everyone was frothing; they just had to get out there, and fast. Like right *now*. Which is exactly when Laird said, "Wait!"

It seemed that Vetea David had locked his keys, along with his sunglasses, in his truck. "No big deal," said the frantic camera teams. "We'll take care of that later. Let's go!"

"No, we'll deal with that now," said Laird. They were a pair of Vetea's sponsor's sunglasses, he explained, and Vetea, one of Tahiti's pioneering professional surfers, had photo incentives as part of his contract. A historic, elaborately documented session like this without those sunglasses could cost him money.

"He's been our generous host," insisted Laird. "So we're going to get him those sunglasses. Somebody find me some wire."

Somebody did, and Laird, turning his mind away from what would most probably be the most dangerous surf session of his life (not to mention the fuming film and boat crews), took a deep breath, slowed his heart rate, and set his focus on getting those keys.

"It wasn't that easy," Laird told me. "The truck didn't have a latch you could unlock. And the keys were in a center console tray."

So Laird fashioned a hook at the end of the wire, then bent out the top rim of the door, inserted his makeshift tool, and began the excruciating process of snatching the key ring out of the console. Which, following much sweaty trial and error, he eventually did, ever so carefully retracting the keys back up and out of the bent-open truck door.

"Jeez, how long did that take?" I asked.

"About twenty minutes," he said. Like, *no big deal.*

But upon reflection, a very big deal.

Consider the essential nature of any breaking ocean wave, from one foot to however high you can count: it is singularly and definitively unique, becoming visible and breaking only once in its watery lifespan, before being absorbed back into the whole. For a surfer, any surfer, there is only that one wave—there will never be another like it. And so being there, in the right place, at the right time, to experience that fleeting moment of existence becomes an endeavor of the utmost importance. Life is built around the effort.

Then consider the technique involved in tow-in surfing. Unlike in conventional surfing, where a surfer sits on the board at a predetermined takeoff spot, waiting for a suitable wave to arrive, the tow surfer is in constant motion, most often circling behind the ski farther offshore, hoping, at the apex of each successive cycle, to be properly positioned for takeoff. Dealing with a vastly more complex set of timing issues necessary to meet that special wave.

Now think about the twenty minutes Laird spent getting those keys out of Vetea's locked truck. Twenty minutes, with the boats and skis and cameras ready, the rest of the team pacing impatiently. I'm sure you can see where this is headed. Because it doesn't take much imagination to realize that if Laird had reached Teahupoo's lineup twenty minutes earlier—or twenty minutes later, for that matter—he might've never been so perfectly positioned to be towed into that wave. *The* wave. His wave.

I ran this concept past Laird.

"Never thought of it that way," he said. "I was just helping a friend."

And with that, for me at least, Lance Burkhart was dead and buried.

Derek Hynd in 2012 in North West, Western Australia. Photo by Ed Sloane

# 5.

## DEREK HYND

### By Jamie Brisick

*"In the 1980 Hang Ten International in Durban, [Derek Hynd] rode a wave to shore and hopped off on the sand, jogging to shave off the speed. When he turned around, his taut urethane leash flung his board at him. It whacked him in the left eye. Derek was so determined to win the heat that he paddled back out and tried to use his injury ('the ooze running down my face was not blood') to psych out his opponent. Only after a water photographer screamed at him to go in did he do so. He was rushed to the emergency room and taken straight into surgery. He'd severed his optic nerve. Two days later, he exited the hospital with a glass eye. He returned to the tour the following year and finished seventh—the first one-eyed surfer in ASP history."*

FORMER PROFESSIONAL SURFER AND REPUTED SURF AUTHOR JAMIE BRISICK tells the story of the eccentric character and surfer that is Derek Hynd. They first met in 1987, when Brisick's sponsor, Rip Curl, hired Hynd to coach the team. His style was unconventional, to say the least. Hynd was a writer himself—his column in *Surfing World* was called "Hyndsight," bylined with a Cyclops logo—with a style that would inspire Brisick's own career in surf journalism.

"Great surfers can be dazzling in the water but terribly boring at the dinner table. Not the case with Derek Hynd," says Brisick. "His mind is as effervescent as his wave-sliding. We've been friends since the late 1980s and I'm still trying to figure him out."

# FOR THE LOVE OF DEREK HYND

In the late 1980s, Derek Hynd worked as a coach and journalist, chronicling the contests and characters on the Association of Surfing Professionals (ASP) world tour. This was a time when surfing was torn between its countercultural roots and the buttoned-up professionalism we know today. The six-week, six-event Euro leg was where surfers let loose, sometimes pulling all-nighters and showing up for their heats still drunk. The final event was in Portugal. One year, straight-edge pro Greg Anderson lost in an early round and wanted to get home to Sydney immediately, but he'd rented a car in Bordeaux—745 miles north—and it needed to be returned there. When he asked around the competitors' area if someone might like to drive it back for him, Derek raised his hand.

Derek had two questions: When did it need to be returned, and did it have unlimited miles?

It needed to be returned in three days, and yes, it had unlimited miles.

Derek pulled out a map of Europe and did the math.

In an issue of *National Geographic*, Derek had read about a coal town in Transylvania known as "The Most Polluted Town in the World." With a curiosity akin to Gomez and Morticia Addams in *The Addams Family*, he just had to see it. That evening, he dropped Greg at Lisbon Airport and continued northeast, crossing seven countries and twenty thousand miles.

Derek gave me a detailed description of his odyssey at the next leg of the tour. We were at a party in Praia da Joaquina, in Florianópolis, Brazil. Many of my fellow pros were either on coke or trying to score some, while Derek was dead sober, with a bag carrying his pens, notebooks, and a dog-eared copy of *Crime and Punishment*. You got plenty of eccentricity in that generation of pro surfing, but you rarely got intellectual curiosity. Derek possessed both. And he still surfed as well as he did when he was a top-ranked pro.

As he lit up with joy describing the soot and char and bleakness, I thought: *Derek's my favorite surfer.*

I knew of Derek Hynd long before I met him: a top-sixteen-ranked pro in the late 1970s, his knock-kneed carves and zingy 360s featured prominently in surf magazines and movies. He rode with a low-slung style, his lithe, rubbery frame much like Mick Jagger's. He had a reputation for being a merciless competitor.

In the 1980 Hang Ten International in Durban, he rode a wave to shore and hopped off on the sand, jogging to shave off the speed. When he turned around, his taut urethane leash flung his board at him. It whacked him in the left eye. Derek was so determined to win the heat that he paddled back out and tried to use his injury ("the ooze running down my face was not blood") to psych out his opponent. Only after a water photographer screamed at him to go in did he do so. He was rushed to the emergency room and taken straight into surgery. He'd severed his optic nerve. Two days later, he exited the hospital with a glass eye.

He returned to the tour the following year and finished seventh—the first one-eyed surfer in ASP history. But Derek had always been more thinker than jock. He retired from competition but continued on tour, this time as a coach and journalist. As a coach, he employed a heavily tactical approach and took great pleasure in watching lesser surfers outsmart giants. As a journalist, he wrote snappy, contentious pieces that often enraged the pros in question. His column in *Surfing World* was called "Hyndsight," and bylined with a Cyclops logo.

Surf magazines were primarily a visual medium. At least 80 percent of the content was photos. Derek's words brought the pages to life in a way that the photos did not. They made me vividly aware of language. And true to the rebel nature of surfing, Derek defied many writing maxims. He did not write simply and directly; he wrote complexly and musically. He called attention to diction and syntax. There were many one-word sentences. As a suburban teen relatively new to surfing, I was rapt. Not only did surfing hold an aesthetic appeal that made me want to swan dive into it, but there was a lingo, there was a jazz to the way you could describe it and think about it.

In a mid-1980s travel piece with teen prodigy Mark "Occy" Occhilupo, Derek kept switching up Mark's name, so that by the end of the piece he's Fergus McOcchilupo. Later I'd see how this perfectly captures the shorthand, inside jokes, and general piss-taking that happens on a surf trip. Observing Occy's idiot savant–ish qualities, Derek describes him as "a potential fool or a potential superstar." (Occy would win the world title in 1999.)

I first met Derek in person in 1986 when I traveled to Australia as a pro surfer. A shaggy fellow given to Blundstone boots, pink shorts, and tweed vests over T-shirts, he was nothing like the puffed-up surfers who huddled in competitors' areas. His shoulders slumped, and his aquiline face wore an expression of perpetual disbelief. He spoke slowly, cryptically. He clutched a gray exercise book and wrote in it constantly.

In 1987, my sponsor, Rip Curl, hired Derek to coach the team. His methods were peculiar. In his exercise book, he transcribed every ride of every Rip Curl surfer's heat, as well as their opponent's. He wrote in tiny, curlicue script, with a race caller's urgency, so that a typical entry would look like this:

<u>JB 2nd</u>: *foamy, late, B hook, A hit float, cuttie roundhouse G+*

<u>RM 2nd</u>: *wide, critical, A layback snap, B+ cuttie, A- reo*
VG FULL ATTACK

*HEAVY PRESSURE ON BOTH—JB NEEDS VG!*[1]

Derek's beachside manner was like Slugworth's in *Charlie and the Chocolate Factory*. He whispered in my ear with a cupped mouth, drew plays in the sand, and then abruptly scratched them out. He told me where to sit, which waves and maneuvers were scoring highest, and what tactics to use. "If you're not up on the first wave, you'll be pushing shit uphill," he'd say. Or, "I hate to break it to you, Jim [he called me Jim], but Occy's the superior surfer. Your only hope is to keep him off the set waves."

Our relationship was humming along, and he'd assisted me in getting a few decent results, when suddenly he went from coach to opponent.

This was at the 1987 Margaret River Pro in Western Australia. In the days leading up to the event, the waves were big and chunky. Among the fifty-odd pros in the water, Derek was a standout. While the top sixteen went up-down,

---

1  Here's a loose translation:
   JB's second wave, a foamy late takeoff, a B-grade hook, an A-grade hit (off the lip), a floater, a roundhouse cutback. Ride should score in the Good-plus range.
   I can't remember who RM was (initials of my opponent.). He caught his critical wave wide, pulled an A-grade layback snap, a B-plus cutback, an A-minus reentry. He fully attacked the wave.
   Now I need a very good (VG) ride.

up-down, he carved long, arcing figure eights in which he'd rebound off the foam in such a low tuck that he seemed to be almost sitting on his board.

When a spot opened up in the trials, Derek jumped on it. He won his first couple of rounds by a large margin. I remember thinking that he could very well win the entire contest. Then I checked the draw and discovered that we were in the same four-man heat.

Our pre-match decorum, whether we wished each other good luck, how we got around the fact that he was supposed to be coaching me—all of it is washed away by a single moment: Derek and I straddle our boards side by side, eyes aimed seaward. The waves are nearly three-times overhead, their broad faces burnished by a light offshore wind. The sun is blinding. The horizon turns dark, signaling a set of waves. We stroke out to meet it. A shimmering, twelve-foot wall stands up perfectly. I'm in position.

Hearts thumping, adrenaline squirting, Derek says, "Gimme this wave, Jim, and I'll buy you fifteen beers."

It threw me. Why *fifteen?* Why not *I'll buy you a beer*, or *a six-pack*, or simply *I'll owe you one?* As I pondered this, Derek slithered to my inside, stole the wave, and knocked me out of the event.

I was sure he was going to take down all the giants; it'd be epic, like something he'd write about—Derek would manifest his victory. But he didn't. He lost a couple rounds later and went back to his coaching and writing as if the whole thing had never happened. Did it change things between us? No. It was a firsthand lesson in something Derek was trying to teach me: that nice guys finish last. That you have to be a shark. That, to borrow a Hynd-ism, "bastard desire" wins.

In the late 1980s, the ASP tour was a relentless ten-country, twenty-five-event affair. Derek and I were frequent traveling partners. A typical evening might see me in one corner of our cheap hotel room, stretching, polishing my board, psyching up for the next day's competition, and Derek in the other, lying on his stomach, headphones on, writing in longhand a piece that was due at the magazine in an hour (he thrived on deadline pressure).

"Have a listen to this, Jim," he'd say, and read me a punchy bit.

In a story titled "The Colors of Madness," Derek describes the beatific afterglow of hot sex with his girlfriend. She gets up to use the restroom and returns languorously to bed. Then Derek gets up to use the restroom. In the toilet he finds a small kernel of shit, "an orphan of her being.… I couldn't possibly flush it." He scoops it up with his hand, brings it back to bed, and holds it out to show her. "Baby," he tells her, "you left me a gift."

In the early 1990s, Derek conceived of "The Search," an ad campaign that, in hindsight (no pun intended), was much more than just an ad campaign. Surfing was in an existential crisis. The '80s had seen an explosion in popularity. Quiksilver and Billabong had reached Midwest department stores. At the 1986 Op Pro in Huntington Beach, attendance was the largest in surf history, escalating into a full-scale riot in which cop cars and lifeguard trucks burned (surfing's Altamont, minus the fatalities). Its bigness raised the question: What exactly was surfing? A sport, an art, a lifestyle? "The Search" attempted to provide an answer.

At that time, Derek was doing marketing work for Rip Curl, which was suffering along with the rest of the surf industry. He described a meeting with the executives and the marketing team in which they were trying to come up with ways to revive the brand.

Three-time world champion Tom Curren was Rip Curl's greatest asset. Derek knew that Tom still had many good years left in him, and that they'd be best realized away from the contest arena. He also knew of a highly marketable South African, Frankie Oberholzer, who was a prodigious surfer but a terrible competitor. Derek imagined Tom and Frankie traveling to far-flung locales and riding glorious, sun-kissed waves in the vein of Mike Hynson and Robert August in *The Endless Summer*, and he proposed this in the meeting. The entire room ate it up. When the Rip Curl CEOs asked Derek if he had a name for his brilliant idea, Derek looked to the wall behind their heads. There hung a poster of the extreme skier Glen Plake. The tiny text at the bottom read: *The Search*.

Derek nodded confidently and said, "The Search."

"Bloody genius!" said the CEOs.

One of the early "Search" ads, shot in the Canary Islands, featured a procession of ruler-edged, beautifully shaped waves with not a single surfer in the lineup. It brought us back to surfing's original myth: the perfect, empty wave—it was still out there.

As "The Search" took off, so did Derek. In South Africa, he built a pyramid-shaped house overlooking Jeffreys Bay, one of the world's longest and best waves. He decked the house out with a nearly 90-degree slide that connected his capsule-like bedroom to the living room, where dozens of boards—some bought at garage sales and swap meets, others procured from top shapers and surfers globally—lined the walls.

Every morning he woke at dawn, studied the waves, and selected his board accordingly. A sort of time traveling ensued. His 1973 Lightning Bolt pintail, for instance, conjured yoga, Timothy Leary, Santana's *Abraxas*. His late-1960s Malibu Chip summoned surf nihilist Miki Dora and, perhaps, the Beach Boys' *Pet Sounds*. Derek drew unconventional lines across the waves, often riding high in the pocket at breakneck speed, hair blown back, arms like wings. He'd always been an expressive surfer, but never like this.

Derek Hynd in 2014 at Jeffreys Bay, South Africa. Photo by Alan van Gysen

In 2010, a video was posted on YouTube that not only captivated the surf world but got it scratching its collective chin with what-ifs. In it, Derek takes off on a series of double- and sometimes triple-overhead waves. All appears to be normal at first. He rides in a low crouch, rear hand tickling the wave face. But there's a subtle drift in effect. The usual traction between surfboard and wave is nonexistent. As the clip kicks on, we see Derek slip and slide and drift and careen and ride backward and spin a fit of dizzying 360s—his board has no fins.

"About fifteen years ago, I watched the Daytona 500 live, and wanted that feeling on the high line," Derek told me later. "I got to wonder what it'd be like to deliberately lose friction going as fast as I could but increase the speed. That's what I got a glimpse into when the leading car—green car 66, I think—lost it with the field up its backside, and for a tiny moment put a gap on the chasers until it flipped multiple times. It lost traction, thus friction, and went faster for a flash. With the pack less than a yard behind at two hundred miles per hour high on the speed bank, I saw the shift." Derek was fifty-five at the time.

It's key to understand just how important fins are to surfboards. They provide the bite, the hold, the traction. They are what keeps the board pointing forward. Without fins (or a fin), there is very little to cling to the wave face. Finless, a surfer is not unlike a child sliding down a snow hill on an inner tube.

"When the wave is going super fast, and a board that shouldn't be matching it *is* matching it," he told me, right hand driving an imaginary board across his face, "it leaves you breathless about the potential of where surfing may have gone fifty years ago had the fin never gained such static popularity. I got a wave this year at Jeffreys, a big wave, and I was on it, and the sections were coming toward me, and I wasn't going to make it but I *was* making it, and I was aware of my mouth getting wider and wider open, and the wind getting in my mouth, and I was conscious of knowing that the board's out of control.... *No, it's in control! Whoa, what's happening to me? What's happening to the board?* It was at a point of maximum velocity. I'd passed through some sort of barrier."

This was in 2009. Derek and I were standing in the shed behind his mother's house in Newport Beach, on the Northern Beaches of Sydney. There was a rack full of surfboards. Derek pulled out one of his new finless boards—or more like *old* finless boards. Browned from the sun, it's crude and asymmetrical, the tail slashed with grooves—this is what creates traction, though not even close to the degree that a fin does. Derek explained that it was a work in progress, that he often scrapes away at the hull with a file, reshaping the board to suit the conditions.

I told him that it looked like something Fred Flintstone would ride.

Derek spoke with a mad-professor wonder: "Picture a pro sportsman of many years in the game suddenly changing dramatic tack, a golfer reducing his club head sizings to just about nothing in order to increase the speed of his swing through the air as a way to spark a new method, or Federer not being content to use the small Sampras head but reducing it to such a 1960s extent where the racket through the air is quicker and the ball off a reduced sweet spot could be harder, faster. Every sport is at the point in history and technology where delivering outcomes like these are possible, right? Only it takes someone with a level of knowledge and commitment to pull it off. It means abandoning the past to work on future outcomes, never going back. And out there today in the conservative world of pro sport, no one can leap, the pioneering mindset is gone."

We strapped the boards to the roof of Derek's '78 Holden Kingswood and headed down a suburban lane toward Barrenjoey Road, the coastal road that snakes through the Northern Beaches. Newport has a neighborly, small-town vibe. As we puttered through the shops (the main drag stretched about a half mile), Derek waved to friends. We passed the Newport Peak, Bilgola, Avalon, and Whale Beach—short, cove-like beaches replete with rocks, points, and outcroppings, the stuff that makes this stretch of coast a surfer's wonderland. We arrived at Palm Beach, an upscale neighborhood that is to Sydney what Malibu is to Los Angeles. We passed the creepy-looking home that belonged to Australia's most famous dominatrix, Madame Lash, whose A-list clientele allegedly included Rupert Murdoch. We parked in a grassy spot a few doors down from the palatial estate that Nicole Kidman rented over Christmas holidays.

"Looks alright," said Derek, pointing to a frothy blue wave.

We suited up, pulled our boards from the roof, and headed to the water. It has been said that great surfers' mastery spills over into the way they hold their board, the way they walk across the sand. Derek was all of this, though his was not a prideful Superman strut but more a languorous, almost yawning stroll. Ditto the way he read the ocean with a glance and timed his paddle out perfectly, zigzagging through the breaking waves and arriving to the lineup with dry hair.

On a wave, he was dazzling. Stroking his way to the frothing crest, he dropped in late, at an angle. His pop from prone to feet was an effortless, split-second transition. He never fully stood up; he rode in a low crouch, knock-kneed, right hand gripping outside rail, left hand aimed knifelike straight ahead. He rode high on the face, dancing in and around what's called the trim line, the vertical spot where the wave sucks up and pitches. His "free friction" approach was obvious: he did little sideslips, his tail pointing shoreward for a couple of seconds and then correcting. He went much faster than any of the couple dozen surfers in the water—while they went up and down and drew figure eights, Derek drew a straight line. Just watching him brought on that weightless, heart-in-mouth feeling.

His next wave was a short, bowly right. He popped to his feet and, in a pouncing crouch, slipped right into a 360. It was not a quick spinner but rather a slow, drawn-out 90 degrees to 180 degrees to a full circle, in which he rode sideways for a suspended couple of seconds, as if to revel in the anchorlessness, as if to play with the fact that he was at the wave's whim. "Play" is the key word. Derek compared free friction to Formula One, and this is true. But my immediate response when I first saw him riding finless on YouTube was that it was childlike, the kind of jury-rigged thing you might see a nine-year-old in a poverty-stricken country do on, say, a discarded piece of plywood. It seemed like the ultimate rebellion against middle age.

Derek reinforced this idea after his surf. Board under arm, face crusted with salt, he stopped to have a chat with his mates, all Palm Beach regulars who had designed their lives around the surf. He changed out of his wetsuit and hung it over a fence that abutted a $10-million mansion. He sat on the grass, barefoot, and inspected his board. A friend walked over, and he and Derek talked about the building swell in shorthand that to the non-surfer would sound like a foreign language. Derek held his hand up to check the wind.

"Sou'westerly," he said. "Could be really good tomorrow morning."

"Meet me at the BP station," said Derek, when I telephoned him to make plans to meet up. This was in 2012, on another trip to Australia. "You'll hit it right as you arrive into town."

Byron Bay, Derek's adopted home for the last couple of years, was a seaside community teeming with surfers, yogis, hippies, and vegans. Even the neighborhood gas station sold fresh local fruit. Derek pulled up in his Kingswood. "Follow me," he said, and I trailed him in my rental car. We turned

into an industrial park and arrived at a cul-de-sac. We entered a studio full of spankin' new boards. As in all surfboard factories, there was the incessant whine of the shaper's planer and the brain-cell-frying scent of fresh resin. Upstairs, on wooden racks and under bright lights, were the first seven of Derek's limited-edition Seven Squared series boards. Brightly colored, with long grooves carved into the tail, they would command a hefty price tag. Derek explained that it was a labor of love: "In case you're wondering, I haven't made a cent."

"F-F-F-F," I said, reading the four Fs on the rail as if they were an acronym.

"No, it's '*ffff*.' That's the way these boards sound on the wave." Derek—black sneakers, blue jeans, Hawaiian shirt over tee—raised one up from the tail and inspected the bottom.

I asked him about his surfing goals.

"It's about FFFF on most levels, I guess. Leaving fettered things behind, testing possibilities, seeing how far I can get before conking out. The future sits in the past for most people." Derek set the board down, slipped his hands into his pockets. "For me, a turning point was seeing two-thirds of my surfing pals fall to the lure of drugs in my hometown when I was right on sixteen years old—and it happened one morning. They never came back. Their souls were gone. Four of us were left, and we just looked at each other: *What's happened?* Since that morning, I think I've been steeled not to get my soul ripped away by drugs or work or other life pitfalls. I've engineered FFFF well enough to never want to go back to the pivot of fins, and maybe that's a metaphor for the standard crutches that people fall back on as the years wear on."

We hopped in Derek's car and drove to a nearby health food store for lunch. A portrait of Sai Baba hung on the wall. A dreadlocked mother breast-fed her baby in the bulk foods aisle. Derek ordered only a carrot juice. He's known for his austere diet. Like a fireman or paramedic, it's as if he wanted to be ever ready for that ephemeral swell.

I asked him how he paid the bills. "Nothing has changed since I left university," he said. "Writing, mostly. Other stuff at stages within the surf industry, but the staple has been to put pen to paper. I was a 'last Mohican' with pen to paper, by the way. I didn't like the keyboard, because I lost the ability to tell through the way my ink looked on a sheet of paper when I was thinking just right to complete a story. The ease of the stroke told me when I was on song or not."

After lunch we drove about a half-mile up the road to The Pass, Byron Bay's most popular surf break. Derek stepped out of the car and found a spot under a tree to scan the waves. He dipped into a squat that looked excruciating on the knees, and stayed there. The Pass is a long, sandy point break with a double-mounded rock clump at the tip that resembles an airbrushed painting you'd find hanging on a stoned surfer's bedroom wall, a nirvana of sorts. But today the wind was onshore, and the waves had lost their perfect shape.

"The bank just got blasted away," said Derek, referring to the recent cyclone that had ravaged the northern New South Wales coastline.

Still, there were plenty of surfers in the water. A vibrant thirtyish girl toting a longboard sauntered past and nodded to Derek. He smiled. Derek is hailed as a visionary genius around these parts. On The Pass's endless, forgiving waves, he has done much of his free-friction test piloting. For a couple years, Derek was romantically involved with a surfer girl half his age. They'd shared waves. He'd called her his favorite surfer. When I first heard about it, I thought, *Right, makes perfect sense. You ride finless, spend your days chasing waves, have a spriteish glint in your eyes. You are more akin to a twenty-four-year-old than a woman your own age.* When it ended, he was heartbroken. But he's always favored the brief and twinkling over the long and dependable.

"Who knows why we're here," said Derek. "It's whatever turns you on, whatever makes you happy. *That's* the essence."

On a chilly night in October 2013, a black livery car pulls up in front of Pilgrim Surf + Supply in Williamsburg, Brooklyn. The rear door swings open, and out steps Derek. He wears black Blundstone boots, black jeans, a black T-shirt, and a black wool blazer. With help from the driver, he pulls from the rear a duffel bag and a coffin board bag. Derek looks road-weary, his long, tousled hair in his eyes. He has just returned from a stint at Jeffreys Bay. In a few days, he'll go to Chile. He heaves his board over his shoulder and enters the shop, where a few dozen fans await him. An image of the wandering minstrel—Johnny Cash, Bob Dylan—comes to mind.

Pilgrim regularly hosts movie screenings and product launches. Tonight is a Q&A with Derek—I'll be handling the "Q" part. When Derek enters the room, he's greeted with shy nods and whispers. People are not sure how to approach him. The ice is broken when a gray-haired fellow quotes back to him a sentence he wrote for *SURFER* magazine in 1993. Another guy—young, hipsterish—tells how he knows a guy who went down his slide at Jeffreys Bay. Derek is humble in his eccentric way. He loves to chat.

Derek and I are shown to chairs. I have no idea how the night's going to go. Derek can be verbose and colorful. He can just as likely be taciturn and aloof. Surfers from Derek's generation are often suspicious of the "fashion factor" in surfing, and though I can personally vouch for Pilgrim's authenticity, I can easily see Derek feeling like a dancing seal expected to perform for a clueless crowd. Halfway through my first question, though, Derek picks it up and runs with it. He does this for the entire Q&A. When I ask what surfing has taught him, he says, "To never tread water, to let the imagination reign, to be able to leave the drudge bullshit that happens on land behind."

In my twenty years of writing about surfing, I have witnessed a recurring theme. Great, charismatic surfers often go on to become excellent storytellers. Their bodies grow wide, their cutbacks and off-the-lips pick up new kinks, but their stories about a perfect day at Pipeline back in, say, 1988 get more vivid and compelling with time. Derek's stories—drawing laughs from the room—do this. But he's anything but portly. And what he's doing in the water today is more innovative and exciting than what he did at age twenty.

After the Q&A, Derek is flocked by admirers. He drags them downstairs to the back room, where he unsheathes his finless boards. A kind of shoptalk ensues. Derek explains the grooves and ridges he carves into the hull of his boards. He runs his hands over the rails and hull as if caressing a body. With animated gestures, almost pantomiming, he explains how it moves across the water: "Your front foot's here, back foot's there.... You're constantly lifting up and down.... This edge gives extreme bite off the bottom turn…"

One of the admirers asks what he loves most about finless surfing.

Derek raises his finger to his chin. His obsession is palpable. After a long beat, he says, "It's like going back to when you were thirteen—liking to wipe out, being amazed at making a wave, being super stoked that there's a variable involving any possibility on a wave face. There's nothing structured about riding without a fin. It makes me wonder what I was doing for thirty years of my life just taking off on waves and running to a pattern."

*Shaun Tomson in 1975 at Off the Wall, Oahu, Hawaii. Photo by Dan Merkel*

# 6.

# SHAUN TOMSON

## By Chris Carter

*"Over the next three North Shore Hawaiian winters, Shaun and a handful of surfers changed the way all of us thought about surfing, the way surfing was photographed, the way it would become a legitimate professional sport. Suddenly there was a pro tour, and more prize money than the gypsy surf circuit had ever dreamed of. Shaun won the world championship in 1977, the second year of former competitor Fred Hemmings' new International Professional Surfing tour. But it hadn't been easy. He and Australian Wayne "Rabbit" Bartholomew had come right down to the wire. Their rivalry would last for years, with Rabbit becoming world champ the following season, in 1978.*

*Another Aussie, Mark Richards, with his own idiosyncratic style, won the next four years in a row. With the '76 world champ, Peter Townend, fellow Aussie Ian Cairns, and Mike Tomson, Shaun's older cousin, they are the core of what historians now call surfing's Greatest Generation."*

South African Shaun Tomson is considered one of the most influential surfers of all time. A pioneer of modern-day surf style, he rode infamous waves like Pipeline, Backdoor, and Off the Wall along Oahu's North Shore with a radical new attitude and style. Chris Carter, award-winning Hollywood writer, producer, and creator of *The X-Files*, was at the time an editor at *Surfing* magazine. He first profiled Tomson during that time, and now, forty-plus years later, profiles him again.

# I WILL

Early in my Hollywood career in the mid-1980s, we were auditioning actors for a TV pilot I'd written at NBC. In the middle of the session, the casting director got a call from an agent asking if we might take a look at a client of hers. The agent knew there wasn't a part in the script for a twenty-year-old guy, but would we just meet him? "He's on the studio lot and, y'know, you might have something down the line."

Ten minutes later, the door opens and a slender young man is invited in. He's got an easy smile, good hair, and a light in his eye.

The cliché about producers and directors being stone-faced tough customers is far from the truth, in my experience. Every time an actor reads for a part, you're desperate for them to be the one. You're hoping you can take them to the next level, the network, where they'll agree with you and allow you to book the part. This rarely happens. Money is at stake, and since the network execs are already hedging their bets that you're going to fail, they're always second-guessing you. And themselves. The process is blunt, crude. I once witnessed the head of a network turn to his associates after an actress had left the room and pose a question: "Would *you* fuck her?" There were women execs in the room too, but this was the mid-'80s—almost forty years ago, when that bullshit flew.

And this kid who just walked in the door? He has something. A presence. Maybe a slight drawl. And he keeps flashing that sly smile. I can feel the women in the room take special notice. And the actor can, too, because he knows what he's selling. He's cute. And he knows he's cute. But cute only lands you on soap operas. This is something else entirely.

We say our hellos, where-are-you-froms, where'd you go to school? University of Missouri.

Show biz is rife with sexy young beach boys and California girls. From Arkansas or Alabama. But if this guy can act, it doesn't matter if he's from Moose Jaw. He's going places.

So it was when Brad Pitt left the room.

So it was with Shaun Tomson, only his instantaneous vault from obscurity to stardom wasn't onto a movie screen (that would come later); it was onto the pages of *Surfing* magazine.

It was 1974. I and my few high school friends who surfed had enjoyed a summer of freedom and warm waves after graduation. In September, I passed my tryout and made my college baseball team, but I missed the freedom and the surf, so I quit and focused on becoming a goof-off and a mediocre student.

That winter, the photos started appearing, and then a cover shot of Shaun perfectly positioned in a perfect tube. Inside were water shots of him doing powerful cutbacks, and the sequences didn't lie; he was pulling them off. He was making those perfect tubes—with a low, wide, self-confident, and idiosyncratic stance. It gave the impression that not only was he good—he never fell.

In the stories, he said incredible things like, "Time is expanded in the tube." Or, "Sometimes I feel I can bend the wave to my will."

We had never heard of Shaun Tomson. He was from South Africa. Maybe we remembered from *The Endless Summer* there were perfect waves down there, but to us it might as well have been Moose Jaw. And he was our age and ripping Hawaiian surf, which was either exciting or depressing; I don't remember. We were lucky just to make a good bottom turn. What I do remember: not missing baseball at all.

Shaun Tomson was an overnight sensation everywhere but in South Africa. By 1974, for three years running, he'd won the Gunston 500,[2] a local pro contest that his father cofounded. And 1974 wasn't the first time he'd gone to Hawaii. His dad had taken him when he was thirteen, for his bar mitzvah, and they'd stayed all winter. As the stories started to come out, it began to make sense. He'd gone back to Hawaii several times to challenge himself in big, powerful surf. He'd had a photo in *SURFER* the previous winter, but they'd misnamed him in the caption, calling him Australian Terry Fitzgerald, whose curly blond hair looked nothing like Shaun's. Shaun had just been waiting for his close-up.

And they did indeed have good waves in South Africa—he'd been surfing them since he was nine. His dad actually encouraged his surfing. He bought him boards, coached him. My dad told me to get a job.

Over the next three North Shore Hawaiian winters, Shaun and a handful of surfers changed the way all of us thought about surfing, the way surfing was photographed, the way it would become a legitimate professional sport. Suddenly there was a pro tour, and more prize money than the gypsy surf circuit ever dreamed of. Shaun won the world championship in 1977, the second year of former competitor Fred Hemmings' new International Professional Surfing tour. But it hadn't been easy. He and Australian Wayne "Rabbit" Bartholomew had come right down to the wire. Their rivalry would last for years, with Rabbit becoming world champ the following season, in 1978. Another Aussie, Mark Richards, with his own idiosyncratic style, won the next

---

2  A professional surf contest held in South Africa from 1969 to 1999, originally called the Durban 500; it was a world pro circuit mainstay in the '70s, '80s, and part of the '90s.

four years in a row. With the '76 world champ, Peter Townend, fellow Aussie Ian Cairns, and Mike Tomson, Shaun's older cousin, they are the core of what historians now call surfing's Greatest Generation.

Shaun never won another world championship. He came close in 1981, was always a threat, but like a lot of the pros, he was chasing evolving board designs, when it was his original quiver that had given him the advantage on the North Shore. For the next decade though, he was one of the most photographed surfers in the world. And one of the most charismatic. Filmmaker Bill Delaney centered his movie *Free Ride* around Shaun and Rabbit. Both smart, handsome, and keen to do the hard work it took to immortalize the winter of 1975.

Legendary surf photographer Aaron Chang recalls watching them at Off the Wall, a surf spot Shaun and his crew practically created, wedged within the inventory of breaks from Haleiwa to Velzyland. "Shaun would be out and had this amazing instinct—he always knew where the best waves were going to be. I watched him working closely with Dan Merkel and the big film camera he was using for *Free Ride*. I'd never seen that: a surfer actually working with a photographer." Lights, camera, action.

Another legend, Jeff Divine, lived in a house right at Off the Wall during the winters of 1974 through 1977. The spot came to be known as Kodak Reef because it was so crowded with camera men—and women. When it was on, OTW was ground zero for the tube-riding revolution that Shaun was conducting, right off Jeff's front porch.

"My bedroom window was next to the public beach right-of-way," Jeff says. "For days on end, I'd be woken to the early riser surfers and their noises. I could check the surf through their voices: excited, arguing, disinterested, or mum."

When the conditions were right, Jeff would hear guys outside his window hooting, shouting superlatives at the tubes being ridden. "I'd bolt upright and lunge for my camera gear. Shaun Tomson was in the water. He was the best surfer in the world."

In the beginning, Shaun and the crew had done it for the prestige and the notoriety, to be considered the greatest. In the forty years since, that remains unchanged. Even with the money, the corporate sponsorships, the new breed of hellmen who ride giants—pro surfing results may make history, but photos and videos make reputations.

This has all been well-documented, though younger surfers may not appreciate it, or know they owe a debt. *Tempus fugit*. Surfing the pastime hasn't changed. Surfing the sport has changed radically.

I did come to appreciate the significance, and write about it. My senior year of college I did an internship at *Surfing* magazine. That gave me season tickets. I hadn't intended to, but I stayed for five years. Looking back, those were some of the most important years of my youth.

Shaun retired from pro surfing in 1990, though that's hardly the final chapter. Sparked by a new fever for surfing and for surf fashion in that era, beachwear brands catered to tastes they had created. The pros reaped sweet sponsorships; the corps hauled in multimillions. But a few pros weren't having it and created their own gigs, looking to capitalize.

Fittingly, in 1979, Shaun started Instinct. His cousin Mike started Gotcha. Raised together, competitors in the water, they were both driven to excel but temperamentally were strikingly different young men. They were their own brands, selling themselves. Shaun posed for his print ads as surfers came to know him: confident, handsome (so good-looking, he modeled for Calvin Klein and posed somewhat feyly for fashion photog Bruce Weber), untouched by the coral reefs he surfed over. Maybe a little brooding. He was a surfer god.

MT was selling himself too. Not exactly the legend his cousin was, he appeared in Gotcha ads with younger pros he sponsored, shirtless, laughing it up—with a beautiful girl in a swimsuit crawling through the shot in front of them. MT was selling sex. Shaun wasn't.

Gotcha was an international success. Instinct couldn't seem to catch a good wave. Shaun lost control of the company in the early '90s, and suddenly he was a former pro surfer knocking on doors. Literally. A father now, with a wife and son, he couldn't get a job in the industry. The designer, if not the architect, of the sport's very image. A former world champ. Unhireable.

MT spun off a division of Gotcha called More Core Division. It was brash, in your face. Bad boy. And it ended up being a sort of last gasp for its owner. Shaun's older cousin became a victim of excess and the party and drug culture the sport had tried to live down in the '70s and '80s. Shaun was his opposite: anti-drug and committed to the cause.

I once saw the enmity between them play out with a North Shore board shaper named Bill Barnfield. He'd made guns for both Tomsons, but he'd put Shaun's logo on both boards. MT, who could be volatile, had a near meltdown. This was more than ego; it was some kind of deep childhood shit. Years later, Shaun would bridge their differences trying to save his cousin's life. Shaun eventually landed at Patagonia, stayed two years, and then gave it another shot with a surf clothing company of his own called Solitude. His wife, Carla, did the design work, and they were successful until the financial meltdown of 2008 caused their near ruin. A friend of a friend who admired their work stepped in and saved them. They eventually sold the company, cashed out, and moved on. Some might have questioned Shaun's business smarts at this point.

I'm sitting with a few people in an auditorium at Santa Barbara City College in 2023. Shaun is on stage doing a sound check. Behind him on-screen is an astounding photo of him at Pipeline, riding a monster that's got horrible side chop on the face, a lip obliterated by offshores. It's a wonder he made the takeoff, a miracle if he makes the drop. His body is stretched fully out, wingspan preternatural. He's connected to his board by only his toes. Bannered above the wave are words that don't square with the photo, that don't belong there: *The Harvard Club of Santa Barbara.*

I call out to him from the dark. Could he have possibly made the wave? There exists a sequence by another photographer, he tells me.

He made it.

Harvard alums begin to file into the auditorium. An older guy sits next to me. As if cued, he says, "Let's see what this guy has to say." To a surfer, the photo says it all.

Shaun stalls on the takeoff with a few off-the-cuff remarks about moving into a new house. I'm getting a little nervous for him. Then he cuts back to his PowerPoint presentation, on finding one's purpose in business: What is purpose? What's not? The elements of purpose.

He banks off a section of personal stories. How his dad was bitten by a shark as a young man, dashing his hopes as an Olympic swimmer. How Shaun went back to college after his pro career and got two degrees, the last one in leadership. How he's shared the stage with celebrities like Richard Branson and Malcolm Gladwell.

He pulls into his pro surf stories and shows a slide of himself carving backside, setting up for a classic Pipeline tube, with the words "Do A Good Turn Today." This is the wave he wants you to ride with him.

Shaun is on a goodwill mission. Or rather, an "I will" mission. He wraps up his talk with an exercise: write a series of resolutions beginning with the words "I will" or "I will not." He wants the Harvardians to jot down ten and text them to him. Then he'll post them. Risky business with this crowd. I sense some disinterest. A whiff of toxic positivity.

*Shaun Tomson in 1976 on the Kamahameha Highway at Off the Wall, Oahu, Hawaii. Photo by Dan Merkel*

This idea came to him when a friend asked him to talk to an elementary school class. Shaun proposed the same task to those students: write down your "I wills" and your "I will nots." The kids responded. They were stoked.

Photographer Aaron Chang belongs to a father-son organization called Boys to Men Mentoring, which hosted one of Shaun's motivational talks. "I'd never heard anyone so perfectly articulate the surfing experience," Chang says. "My son and I loved it. It was magnificent."

Shaun's lectures begat four books by him: *Surfer's Code*, *The Code*, *The Surfer and the Sage*, and *Bustin' Down the Door*. All relate Shaun's surfing experiences and life lessons. His bio says two are bestsellers.

I did a profile on Shaun forty years ago. I lived with him for a month on the North Shore. I surfed with him. He was riding a new thruster that Simon Anderson had shaped for him. We dined. Went to nightclubs like Steamers in Haleiwa, dancing to late disco being spun by DJ Georgia Peach. Shaun was a surf star. My intention was to humanize him.

In our interview, he talked about competition and hard work. (He'd hired a coach.) About his pique at surf journalist Drew Kampion's pronouncement of a changing of the guard. A young South African named Martin Potter was winning contests. He'd beat Shaun in their home country. Drew said Shaun's reign was over. Shaun shot back. "People think one contest loss is a convenient way to say your career is over," he told me. "Stuff like that you don't need in your life."

The fact was, he'd had a good run but hadn't won big since 1977.

I hardly humanized him. I lionized him. But I was Shaun's guest in his nice hotel. I gave him the surf-star treatment, because what else was I going to do? Previously I'd lived on the North Shore in a tent.

Shaun was born in Durban, South Africa. Under apartheid. A violent race war was sundering the country. When Shaun was pulling into Hawaiian tubes in '76, Blacks were being murdered by the secret police in the Soweto Uprising. South African sports teams had been banished from Olympic and international competition. Except for surfing. He'd grown up with anti-Semitism in his Jewish community. But all we talked about was surfing. Everything else was superficial.

The real story was staring us right in the face. In a kind of perfect irony, Shaun had left one racist country for another. Hawaiian surfers objected to these white boys from South Africa and Oz hogging not only their waves but all the attention from the media. They were making bold statements. They were "bustin' down the door."

Shaun had made too many magazine covers, won the Hawaiian contests, stuck with his mates. He was articulate and pretty. The North Shore is a lawless place run by violent overlords. There was a rumor that surfer Tommy Castleton had been held on the floor all night with a gun to his head. That Fast Eddie Rothman was behind it. No one wanted to piss off Fast Eddie, of course. His Hawaiian capos had gone to high schools where they had "Kill Haole Day"—*haoles* being white kids. Shaun and the other stars fit the picture.

"They're insular!" Australian surfer Ian Cairns blurted to me in the editorial suite at *Surfing* magazine in 1980, right outside the office where Fast Eddie had walked in and, in effect, threatened editor Dave Gilovich's life if he were to write the "wrong" thing or run the "wrong" photos. It was a war. Some got it worse than others, but Shaun got "false cracked," or hit unexpectedly in the face, by Eddie. Then again by two of Eddie's guys. Shaun doesn't look tough, but he'd served military duty during apartheid. He knew how to shoot a gun. So he bought one.

Shaun loaded the shotgun, ready to use it. He went to bed scared. The North Shore is a scary place, even apart from waves like Pipeline.

Finally a peace of sorts was made, dictated by The Hui, as the gang was known. At a sit-down. Like a Hawaiian star chamber.

I met Eddie once. He shook my hand outside Kammie's Market at Sunset Beach. He was musclebound and expressionless. I wouldn't want to be on any list of his. Who on earth would write about him?

A writer named Chas Smith wrote two hilarious books in which he made Eddie Rothman into a North Shore hero. "Hyper-ironic," they've been called. They're irreverent and sarcastic. Sometimes weird, as when he describes a pro surfer's nipples. Smith has an online magazine with a fellow writer named Derek Rielly. They pick fights, call people names, and act out. It's highly readable. Shaun says even he's not immune.

For all its facets, many say the sport of surfing lacks drama. Something I never understood, but Chas Smith gets it and exploits it. Baiting surfers is part of what he calls his "cinematic life." Matt Warshaw, writer of the excellent *History of Surfing* says he gets a thrill when he hears a surfer has died, and I kinda get what he means. Filming *The X-Files* one day on the top of a building, David Duchovny pointed at a jet overhead and turned to me. "What people really want is to see it blow up and go down in flames," he said. Which is horrible, but somehow explains human nature.

But me? Mostly, I masqueraded as an insider. I spent the bulk of my tenure in the office at the typewriter, rewriting stories about places I'd never been, about surfers I didn't know. William Finnegan, the Pulitzer Prize–winning author of *Barbarian Days* and a surfer who's written for *The New Yorker* since 1984, used to submit articles to me in the '80s. They were great stories, but there were no photos, so they were rejected. Some people never read *Surfing* magazine but for the photos.

Shaun's cousin Mike wrote for *Surfing* mag too. MT was the real insider. He'd shown me where to paddle out my first surf at Sunset Beach. I rode behind him on a solid wave and saw how a real surfer surfed Sunset. It's a wave I hope to never forget.

We had a two-week window to get the editorial ready for each issue of *Surfing*, including typesetting, copy editing, and paste-up. All done by hand then. It wasn't drudge work; it was exhilarating. I credit my success as a TV producer to my job responsibilities there. Twelve issues a year versus twenty-five episodes. I learned to meet a deadline under pressure. I was making $1,500 a month and was denied a raise. My next job paid better.

But as I said, they were five unforgettable years.

Shaun and I now sit opposite each other at lunch for the first time in forty years. Though we live in the same town, I rarely see him. We surf different spots, travel in different circles. We discuss MT, who died a few years earlier of throat cancer. How Shaun had tried to get him help, but he wouldn't take it. "He was either arrogant or in denial," Shaun tells me. Like Shaun, I had tried to help MT, but it was after he'd been busted for cocaine possession. He didn't want my help, either.

We talk about his son's upcoming bar mitzvah, his "barmy." I assume Shaun won't be taking him to the North Shore, and I'm right.

Shaun tells me he's got another idea for a movie, and he's got $2 million. Can I offer any advice about selling it? All roads lead to Hollywood. Shaun has already made a documentary, *Bustin' Down the Door*, after a Rabbit Bartholomew article in *SURFER* magazine in 1975. It's about that groundbreaking year and the tight group of surfers who defined an era. Shaun had asked me to take an early look to see if I had any notes.

Here, again, I've got Shaun in front of me, and here, again, I can't ask him the right questions. Or in this case, the toughest question.

Shaun's son Mathew died playing something called The Choking Game when he was fifteen. There's a moment at the end of *Bustin' Down the Door*

when Shaun breaks down talking about him. It's moving and powerful, and it makes the movie better. I intend to dig into this somehow, but Shaun beats me to it.

He tells me a story about how, after Mathew's death, he didn't want to go surfing. His life fell apart. But a friend convinced him what he needed was to get back in the water. He took Shaun to a spot near Durban he'd never surfed before. Shaun caught his first wave in months, began paddling back out when he saw the sun shining brilliantly through the face of a wave. Tears come in Shaun's telling.

"What's the name of this break?" he asks.

"Sunrise," his friend says.

Just before Mathew died, he had written his father a poem that ended, "the light shines ahead." It's the name of the movie Shaun wants to make, about the bold power of "I will."

Shaun, his wife Carla, and their adopted son, Luke, live on a quiet street in a town where the royals now live. At lunch, when Carla calls him on the phone, he answers, "Hey, baby." Shaun is droll, delivering jokes with serious dramatic pauses. He took acting lessons once. As it happened, prior to our lunch, there was a screening of a remastered *Free Ride*. Sam George interviewed Shaun onstage before the show.

"Rabbit has a vision that one day we could make a living from our passion," Shaun told Sam. "I'm at university, thinking I'm going to be a lawyer or an accountant—"

"Hang on," Sam said. "You revolutionized surfing at one of the gnarliest surf spots in the world, and in the back of your head, you're thinking about being an accountant?" Roars of laughter.

Shaun travels widely now delivering his talks. He thinks of himself as a storyteller rather than a motivational speaker. When he's home he still gets in the water, when most guys our age struggle to get into their wetsuits. He's pushing seventy. We both are. But Shaun still rips.

"He's attacking sections like the Shaun I was in awe of in the late 70s," says fellow former pro Danny Kwock. "Makes me think Kelly Slater will be crushing it until he's 100."

The South Africa kid, inspiring a whole new surf revolution.

*Keala Kennelly in 2017 at Kaimana Beach in Oahu, Hawaii. Photo by John Hook*

# 7.

## KEALA KENNELLY

### By Liza Monroy

"Her fears materialized. She lost three out of four of her sponsors: Vestal, Red Bull, and Spy. It couldn't be called out as discrimination, because 'they wouldn't say, "We're dropping you because you're a lesbian,"' she explains. 'They'd say, "We're dropping you 'cause you're not marketable." It's like, really? 'Cause I just broke this record.... I thought it was based on your results, your wins, and your accomplishments. How am I not marketable? I'm an elite athlete that's doing shit that no other woman was doing.'"

Author and surfer Liza Monroy writes about big-wave rider Keala Kennelly, who has made her name on the most dangerous waves of the world, winning the most prestigious contests in the sport, and holding the distinction of being the first woman invited to the pinnacle of big-wave events, the Eddie Aikau Big Wave Invitational. But when she finally came out as a lesbian, what she feared the most came true. Despite the financial struggles she has faced as a result, the contrast between her achievements and earnings stark, Kennelly has continued to push for women's and gay rights, becoming a pioneering hero in and out of the water.

# WAVES OF CONSEQUENCE: KEALA KENNELLY'S REVOLUTIONARY PATH

On a balmy, birdsong-filled afternoon at Ala Moana park in Honolulu during the summer of 2023, big-wave surfing legend Keala Kennelly sits at a slightly shaded picnic table, occasionally taking bites from a poke bowl while sharing stories from her boundary-breaking career. Branches above rustle in the high tradewinds. Turquoise waves break over coral reefs in the distance. "Ankle-slappers," she calls these waves that, for an average surfer, would be considered fun, an inkling of the fact that Keala is as far from "average surfer" as it gets. With her signature bleached, close-cropped shock of hair and ethereal gold-flecked eyes, Keala has a presence as large and memorable as the giants on which she's made history in her decades of surfing—Teahupoo, Pipe, Sunset, Jaws, Puerto Escondido, and others. She has said that people often expect her to be huge, but at five-foot-six, she's a petite woman who loves charging waves of consequence.

If names speak to identity, hers certainly fits: Keala, a moniker of Hawaiian origin, translates to "the path." Hers has been one of bravery and activism, dedicated to making jaws drop with her full-send drops into Jaws, along with all the other largest, most thrilling, terrifying waves the ocean has on offer. Famed for "sending it" every time, earning her the nickname "Sendelly," Keala has sat deeper, taking off in precarious spots to come up against the edges of what's possible, risking her life and sustaining a litany of injuries in the process while also earning a reputation, as noted in a 2019 *New York Times* article, as "the best female big-wave surfer on Earth."

That article was about the quest for inclusion and equal pay in women's surfing, a struggle in which Keala was also centrally involved. *Surfline* wrote that Keala has "blazed more trails, caught more grief, endured more beatings, tolerated more politics, and done more than any other person this century to advance women's big-wave surfing. And it has taken its toll."

On this blustery, sunny Oahu day, it has been nearly seven months since Keala has surfed, after making history competing at the Eddie Aikau Big Wave Invitational. "The Eddie," as it's known, had one of its most historic moments since its mid-1980s inception: women paddled out for the first time.

For the Eddie to even be held, which has happened only ten times since its inception in 1984, Waimea Bay's waves must reach at least forty feet. When this unusual, perhaps magical, condition occurs, the best forty surfers in the world fly in to compete. The Eddie was a dream, "a once-in-a-lifetime opportunity," says Keala. She was determined to get a "proper bomb."

But early on in the contest, her board broke. She borrowed one—not in her dimensions, nor one she'd ever ridden—from Brazilian big-wave champ Lucas "Chumbo" Chianca. After a couple of smaller waves to get used to it, she sought the biggest on offer.

From years of jockeying with men, Keala knew she had to sit deeper than they were, "even though they're sitting so deep and taking off in such a gnarly spot."

A huge set approached. "Right then I was just like, OK, *this is the moment*," she says. "I whipped and paddled as hard as I could. Right when I got to my feet, the thing jacked. When I look at the photos, it was so freakin' vertical, there was no way I was going to be able to engage a rail. It jacked up and threw me out."

Free-falling for what was seemingly an eternity, "I had some time to contemplate my life and my choices. It felt like I was dropping forever."

She focused on penetrating the water feetfirst, "diver style" (on video, making it look absolutely graceful, given the circumstances). She proceeded to get "really fuckin' pounded, one of the worst beatings ever," held under longer than she can remember.

How does she manage such a wipeout? Breath-holding exercises? "I don't like those," Keala muses. "You gotta relax and pretend you're somewhere else other than underwater getting the shit kicked out of you." She took one more wave to the head before the jet ski swept in. When she got picked up, "They were like, 'That was so gnarly, do you want to go in?'"

Not a chance. "I had so much adrenaline. I was really determined to keep going, get a set, and make it. I said, 'Please take me back out.'"

After a few more waves, "barely staying on my board," she got caught inside during the final heat. "I was scratching to get over this wave—you're going really fast and have a lot of momentum. I went over the top of it, shot up into the air, free-fell over the back of the wave, and landed face-first into the deck of the board. I touched my chin, and there was blood everywhere."

Famed North Shore lifeguard Luke Shepardson, who had also won the Eddie that year, checked it and told her she needed stitches. There were no mirrors, so Keala asked her bewildered girlfriend, "Babe, how is it?" Her girlfriend, trying not to appear horrified, concurred: stitches.

"I really didn't want to go to the hospital," Keala says. "I hate hospitals. The Eddie wasn't over. I didn't want to miss that experience."

She found a medic she'd heard had tended to Chumbo when he got injured during his heat. "She stitched me up in the back of a U-Haul truck." Keala got to stay for the rest of the contest, albeit in searing pain.

With the Eddie in the bag and history made, reality set in. "I was recovering from an injury in my face again, then the winter was over, so I haven't surfed since."

That's a long time for a woman who's been on a board since the womb; Keala's mother surfed until she was about six months pregnant with her only daughter. (Keala has two brothers she's very close with). Her dad is still like a "super-stoked grom," she says. "He probably always surfed more than I do."

Born August 13, 1978, on the island of Kauai, Hawaii, Keala fell in love with surfing when she was five. She knew then that it was what she wanted to do for the rest of her life. In a TEDx talk she gave in 2014, she said, "This was my gift, and the better I got at it, the better I felt about myself."

Peers Andy and Bruce Irons were "like brothers to me," she says. "They actually treated me like a brother, 'cause they'd be mean to me a lot of the time. They were mean to each other, so yeah, I was like family. I grew up in a savage wolf pack of boys. It made me really tough."

Early influences included her godfather, Laird Hamilton, and Kala Alexander, who'd go on to notoriety as the unofficial leader of the "Wolfpak," a surf gang in early-2000s Kauai that went on to enforce etiquette at Pipeline and around the North Shore.

These surfers' feats to outdo one another led Keala to continue to push herself, driven to be their equal, going for "bigger waves, big barrels," she says. "That was what was impressive to them. I wanted to be one of the boys. To be loved, accepted, and respected."

But the boys had a love-hate relationship with young Keala. "If they're out there charging," she observes, "they can beat their chest, but if a girl is going out there and doing the same thing, they felt like, *Am I so masculine and tough if she can do it too?* They'd lash out."

When Keala began competing, there was no girls' division—just an open women's. At age ten, she could compete against women in their twenties and thirties, or against ten- and eleven-year-old boys. She did both.

"The guys hated that I would beat some of them. Andy and Bruce, not so much. I may have beat Andy and Bruce maybe once or twice. Andy wouldn't speak to me for a month. But the other guys, we'd fight for third, fourth, fifth, sixth place. Society taught them—they weren't born with this—that it's shameful to lose to a girl, as opposed to, 'This girl's amazing; she had a great day, and tomorrow it will be your day. Go surf harder; go train harder.' It was embarrassing to be beat by me. All the other guys would talk shit to the guy I beat. They would lash out because of shame and anger."

Having to deal with the toxic-masculinity culture made her strong and relentless, hurt, and served as motivation. As she said in her TEDx Malibu talk, "If we desire something, and then we're told we can't have it, what happens? It makes us desire it more."

Nearing her teen years, she realized that she was gay during the same period she was disinvited by the boys, who had gone on to like "real girls" and no longer wanted her around. When she tried befriending girls, "they would just look at me like, *You're not a real girl; you're a weirdo*. I had a very lonely existence." Being accepted versus being her true self: this inner battle continued for years to come.

Keala continued to push herself surfing, where she'd always excelled. The next step on the path took her from Kauai, from that early life that had revealed surfing was her destiny, to the World Championship Tour. She turned pro at seventeen.

Keala was accepted to the World Championship Tour (WCT) in 1997. Her rise was swift. The following year, she won the Gotcha Black Pearl Women's Pro at Teahupoo ("Chopes," as she and those familiar call it). She describes her beloved Chopes like a lover who "you're so in love with but beats you sometimes," a "thick, hollow, and extremely powerful wave, one of the most dangerous on the planet but also the most beautiful."

She recalls women's surf media pioneer Betty Depolito, aka "Banzai Betty," taking her to Chopes for the first time. "She was like, 'There's this wave in Tahiti; it's right up your alley. I'll take you down there.'"

From the point, Keala explains, you can't really tell how big a wave it is. "You're like, *Is it two-foot? Twenty-foot?* 'Cause it's so far away."

They went out in the boat and got to the lineup. Keala saw "a perfect six-foot-wave barrel down the reef and spit. I went, 'Fuck yes.' I jumped off the boat. I had a brand-new board. I paddled out so excited and sat in the lineup right next to Shane Dorian. He's like, 'Hello KK. Charging, huh?' I didn't know what he was talking about, 'cause I'm like, *Whatever*. It was six-foot. I just saw the set."

She soon realized: it was *not* the set.

"That was not even a normal wave," she says. "It was an in-between-wave wave. I paddled for one of those thinking, *This is it*. It didn't even break. I turned and saw the entire ocean coming for me. I thought I was gonna die. I paddled as fast as I could to get under the lip before it exploded in front of me, just barely made it, and got sucked over the falls. I got pushed down on the

KEALA KENNELLY | 137

reef and held there. I didn't know which way was up, got spun around, grabbed my leash and pulled it like a ladder to try and get to the surface. When I did, there was just a tiny piece of the tail of my board left."

The board had broken into three pieces. "I grabbed the chunk and paddled this little piece of board as fast as I could to the channel. I was shaking. This is before inflation vests, any kind of equipment, no kind of safety…jet skis—nope. There were a couple boats in the water and that was it."

When a women's event there was announced, "I was stoked but a little traumatized. I went back and surfed it. It was pretty big the first day I went back, practicing for the contest. I was nervous as fuck. I got a couple of nice rides, got barreled, and that was just the start of something special."

Keala celebrated three more wins there: 2000, 2002, and 2003, the year she was number one in the WCT rankings. She ended it in second place. Still, it was an epic one. She won the Vans Triple Crown of Surfing, taking the North Shore victories at Haleiwa, Sunset, and Pipeline; the Billabong Pro at Teahupoo; the Roxy Pro in Fiji; and the Turtle Bay Pro in Hawaii. She placed third at the Billabong Pro in Maui. In 2005, she became the first woman to tow-in at Chopes.

Yet, as a closeted gay athlete, she lived in constant fear of being outed and losing her sponsors. Media attention was no help. While pretending to be straight, "I'd have people ask me point-blank if I was a lesbian." In 2002, when she was ranked number four in the world, "I had a *Rolling Stone* interview where the first question was, 'Are you a lesbian?' I would lie. What does that have to do with my surfing? Do you ask Kelly Slater, first interview question, if he's gay? Why are you coming for me?"

It got to the point where anticipating live interviews made Keala clam up. "I would say they could email me questions. I don't want 'gotcha' questions. I felt like I had to lie to save my career. Not being able to be truthful.… I'm a very honest person, so that was killing me."

Then she nearly did die.

While in Costa Rica for a World Qualifying Series event, her appendix ruptured, leaking poisonous bile—a life-threatening infection requiring immediate surgery. Lying on the table, Keala felt regret. Nobody had known the real her.

Upon surviving the ordeal, she knew she needed to be open about who she was. Keala decided to come out, not "swinging rainbow flags in the air," as she puts it, or telling everybody she was gay; rather, she simply stopped hiding.

"I was sick of living this double life on tour, living in fear, and the internalized homophobia and self-hatred I had because I felt like an embarrassment they didn't want visible." A year later, in a relationship with a "proud card-carrying lesbian" (her previous girlfriend was not out), "I started bringing my girlfriend on tour with me," she recalls. "I didn't lie and say, 'This is my friend.' And the reaction was so horrible."

Her fears materialized. She lost three out of four of her sponsors: Vestal, Red Bull, and Spy. It couldn't be called out as discrimination because "they wouldn't say, 'We're dropping you because you're a lesbian,'" she explains. "They'd say, 'We're dropping you 'cause you're not marketable.' It's like, really? 'Cause I just broke this record.… I thought it was based on your results, your wins, and your accomplishments. How am I not marketable? I'm an elite athlete that's doing shit that no other woman was doing." Really, "that was code for, 'You're a lesbian; you're not feminine enough.'" Billabong didn't cut her. But her salary was reduced from six figures in 2007 to, over the course of the next eight years, only a travel budget of $3,000.

The 2014 documentary *Out in the Line-Up*, in which Keala appears, tells the story of gay surfers throughout the industry and the world who have had similar experiences. Being gay "is just one part of who I am," Keala says in her interview. "The way I express myself best is through surfing, not who I'm sleeping with."

She took second place at the Billabong Pro in Maui and a team gold at the 2007 Summer X Games. But with disc issues in her back from injuries, her ranking slipped from second in the world to top five, then top ten. (Up until 2007, she maintained a spot within the top ten of the rankings by the World Surf League's predecessor, the Association of Surfing Professionals.)

Injuries coincided with the developing financial crisis. "With the economy doing so poorly, it was cheaper to run an event in Huntington Beach rather than build a scaffolding out on the reef in Tahiti or Tavarua. A lot of those locations and epic waves meant expensive infrastructure. They were cutting back." With budgets shrinking, "they took away Chopes, they took away Fiji, and they took away Sunset—they took away all the waves that I would excel in. All the events that I would win were gone, replaced with small-wave beach breaks that I am terrible at." Keala's heart, for the first time, fell out of her lifelong passion.

An opportunity showed her the time to move on had come. She was offered a role on the HBO series *John from Cincinnati* (she played Kai, a surf shop employee), created by David Milch.

"I took that as a sign," she says, "of, *You're not happy right now. And you can't even be who you are. And you have this amazing opportunity to go do something else.* I think if that show hadn't presented itself, I probably would have stayed on tour, because what else are you gonna do? You've dedicated your

*Keala Kennelly in 2012 at Peahi, Maui, Hawaii. Photo by Richard Hallman*

whole life to this, and I found out the hard way, when I lost all my sponsors. It was like, *OK, now what do I do? How do I make money?*"

The show ran for a year. In 2008, Keala slammed into a rock bottom as hard as Chopes's reef: "The TV series got canceled. I'd left the tour, all my contracts were up, I'd come out as a lesbian, and the economy was tanking. At that point I just had a mental breakdown of, *What am I gonna do?*"

Unlike many, she was stronger and more confident in larger surf. She describes the thrilling sensations of surfing big waves as "impossible to act like it's not there" after you've felt the absolute rush of it, the heightened feeling of being alive trumping fear: "There'll forever be a gnawing at your soul telling you there's something more."

She'd seen Dave Rastovich and "all these other guys who don't do contests fly to exotic locations, surf nothing but epic waves," she says. "'Free surfers' that surf for photos. I said, 'I want to do *that*.'" But she had to fund her swell-chasing. "If I got photos or did something spectacular, [Billabong] might pay it back. That's how I got into credit card debt."

As a female big-wave free surfer pre–social media and digital photography, she encountered workplace discrimination yet again: photographers weren't shooting women. "I'm spending all this money flying to Indonesia and Australia and Tahiti and all these other places to get photos and just hoping that the guys are out there with their photographers, and that their photographer is going to get some pics I can then get to my sponsors to use in ads or get them into magazines."

Getting a double-page spread in *SURFER* magazine from a trip to Puerto Escondido helped. "That's when I started towing in to some epic waves at

Chopes and getting a lot of exposure from that." Ironically, her salary never went back up. "It went the opposite direction" as she kept chasing swells, starting to ride bigger and bigger waves, incentivized by what it took to get into magazines. "The only way I could seem to get a photo in men's magazines was if I rode a really huge wave, because they'd never seen a female ride a wave like this. That seemed like the only way I could break in: just keep charging bigger."

In 2010, Keala won the first women's big-wave contest, the Nelscott Reef Big Wave Classic in Oregon. Only six women competed. "I hate cold water," she says. "But I was like, *This is the opportunity they're giving women to compete in big waves. I have to go.* And I won. I was stoked. But there was no prize money."

Three years later, she was inducted into the Surfing Walk of Fame in Huntington Beach and the Action Sports Hall of Fame in San Diego and won the Billabong XXL Women's Performance Award. In 2016, she won the Pure Scot Barrel of the Year award at the Big Wave Awards—basically the Oscars of big-wave surfing—for her Chopes barrel on July 22, 2015. It's an award not divided by gender.

When she won the Red Bull Magnitude Biggest Wave Award for the 2020–2021 Hawaiian winter big-wave season, in her acceptance speech she thanked "everybody in my life that told me 'you can't do that because you're a woman.' That drove me to dedicate my life to proving you wrong, and it's been so damn fun."

At the same time, her earnings did not come close to matching her achievements. Her credit card debt totaled nearly $70,000 for getting herself to the big waves. Paddling out in a kayak when men had boats. Begging guys to whip her in when she had no jet ski.

There was an uncanny irony in Keala becoming the first woman invited to the Eddie in 2017 (though the contest didn't take place until 2023). "I was making history, and nobody was willing to sponsor me. That gave me a lot of self-worth issues at that time, because it was just like, *I'm worthless*. I'm achieving all these milestones but making nothing for it. It was so confusing to me. That should have been the year I was getting paid the most and I got nothing."

"Everybody thinks I'm rich," she says. "Everybody thinks I have a beachfront house on the North Shore. They just assume. I'm proud of my legacy, but it's been a hard road. For a lot of women, it's grit, it's struggle."

Little known about Keala was that she was living, at the time, landlocked—in St. Louis, Missouri, where she'd moved trying to make a relationship work. (The former couple shared a son to whom Keala does not have a biological claim.) She worked odd jobs—serving in cafes, painting houses. She jumped at opportunities to chase swells, acknowledging the danger of not surfing "for long periods of time," then jumping right back in at the first big swell at Jaws. "At one point I was like, *How did this become my life?*" she says. "Working minimum-wage jobs away from the ocean—what wrong turn did I take?"

When the relationship ended, she moved to Los Angeles to be on a coast but still closer to her son than she would have been in Hawaii. In LA, she drove for Uber, worked for Postmates and at a poke shop. Then, she says, her ex "started systematically cutting me out of [my son's] life." Able to sustain hours of conversation with laser-sharp focus and nary a pause, Keala falls silent, this weighing heavily. How did she cope?

"I just kept going."

By 2016, she and her "big-wave sisters"—Bianca Valenti, Paige Alms, and Andrea Moller—had had enough. The inequities they faced led them to fight for women's inclusion and equal pay. Teaming with activist and then–San Mateo harbor commissioner Sabrina Brennan and attorney Karen Tynan, the group cofounded the Committee for Equity in Women's Surfing (CEWS), fighting for and ultimately winning equal pay for women in pro surfing.

Mavericks was the central battleground in the fight for a women's division and equal pay in the competition. Brennan, who served two consecutive four-year terms as a harbor commissioner in San Mateo County (which encompasses Mavericks) from 2012 to 2020, showed that gender discrimination in contests that took place on public lands was illegal. Making the push for change at Mavericks was a strategic move resulting in a law requiring that "any competition held on California state land, including the oceanfront, must award equal prize money for all athletes at all participant levels, regardless of gender, as a condition of receiving a lease or permit." Women needed to be included and paid equally for the event to be permitted.

On the Hawaiian end of the push for inclusion and equal pay for female athletes in pro surfing, Banzai Betty—who'd taken Keala to Chopes that first time—played a central role. Full circle.

After years of letter-writing and bureaucracy, the timing of the first surf contest to offer equal cash prizes for women aligned with the #MeToo movement. It took place at Jaws.

Keala won.

The Jaws event being the first for equal pay is why she "just went out there and sent it, harder than I ever had," she says. "It was so big, windy, and lurchy that day. It was my dream to win a world title. Even though I didn't do it on the Championship Tour, I finally won a big-wave world title and got equal pay for the first time."

The same year, she and her big-wave sisters competed for equal prize money—$25k per winner—at Mavericks.

"When you're the one doing the firsts, there's no blueprint for how to reward somebody," she says. "There's no formula for what the value is in that yet. I think about the women that started competing on the world surf tour for no money, for five hundred dollars total prize money. The trailblazers never really reap the benefits. They put in the groundwork."

As witness to the next generation reaping the rewards of what the original CEWS team accomplished, Keala has received the satisfaction of watching the culture shift, if not of reaping concrete rewards. "I know that my contributions have changed the sport, changed the world."

Keala was recognized with the title she'd worked for her entire career: a world championship, becoming the big-wave tour's first openly gay athlete to win. She gave a powerful acceptance speech in front of the whole surfing industry, a moving moment. The story ends with an asterisk, however: Keala had referred to herself as the first openly gay world champion, but that was technically longboarder Cori Schumacher. Keala conducted online research prior to the speech but hadn't found this, and regrets that she "pissed off Cori."

"I should have worded it differently," Keala says. "The sentiment I was trying to make was, 'I'm an LGBT athlete, I'm proud to be out, to be able to have this accomplishment and not have to hide,'" she explains. Regardless of who was "first," what was clear in contrast to Keala's earlier experiences was how much had changed, thanks to both Cori and Keala—and to all the trailblazers willing to risk themselves to move the needle, be true, and make social progress.

Amidst long-awaited victories in public arenas of the surfing industry and society, a deeply personal struggle came to a head. Her whole life, Keala experienced mood swings and depressions but "never recognized that as a symptom," she says. "I guess that's just my personality. I just get shitty. That's how I was."

Two weeks into a major depressive episode after her fortieth birthday, she received news of the historic win. "I woke up after being in bed for almost two weeks and saw an email from [World Surf League CEO] Sophie Goldschmidt to let us know first before they made the announcement that the women were going to be getting equal pay—not just us big-wave women but all women, all platforms. I'd been working on that for years. I should have been over the moon, I should have been elated. But my first thought was, *OK I've fulfilled my purpose. I can probably kill myself now*. And I was like, *How can that be your first thought? You need help*."

She reached out to her mother, who told Keala about a bipolar-disorder history in their family. The highs and lows and extremes suddenly made sense in this new light.

"I'm sure some of my best surfing performances happened when I was manic," Keala says. She saw a psychiatrist, who diagnosed her with bipolar II disorder and prescribed medication for it. Within her first month of taking it, Keala noticed a positive shift. Her diagnosis and treatment brought an answer to a mystery: "I felt devastated, but such a sense of relief that I had a name for this monster that had been plaguing me my entire life."

Having fought for women and LGBT athletes, Keala now had another social quest that went beyond herself: destigmatizing mental illness.

"When I went public, I think probably a lot of people were like, not very surprised," she says matter-of-factly. "Like, 'Oh that makes a lot of sense. Have you seen the waves she hurls herself into? We've always thought she's had a couple screws loose! That tracks for her.'"

As a world-champion big-wave surfer and a DJ, actor, activist, and entrepreneur, Keala is, above all, a showperson, no matter her medium. And not just any show will do. It must be spectacular. A show nobody would soon forget. These days, Keala is more likely to be performing behind her turntables than at Teahupoo, earning more cash in a few hours from tips than she made surfing in the last year.

"I've got a DJ booker that books me on corporate jobs," she says on a Saturday afternoon on the pool deck of the Prince Hotel in Waikiki. "Those pay really well. They'll fly me to Maui. I'll DJ an event at the Grand Wailea." She is given her own hotel room and is well-compensated—a stark contrast to being excluded on tour after undergoing major facial surgery. A luxury hotel versus Mother Nature's most unforgiving waves is about as different as it gets. "People wonder why I haven't been surfing," she says. "And I'm not injured!"

"The last couple years, it's been more wipeouts than makes," she says. "That's happening more than the rush of an incredible ride, and it used to be the opposite. I'd get that rush of getting that incredible ride and not wiping out—but injury after injury, more and more wipeouts, the instability of my back leg [An injury she sustained at Jaws resulted in her "Wipeout of the Year" award. It ripped her leg out of its socket and tore the labrum in her hip.]—the ratio has flipped. I'm not getting the ride or the monetary reward right now. I'm just getting my ass kicked for free, which isn't fun.

"I got to experience so much cool shit," she says of her surfing career. "Sometimes I miss that. Not so much the contests. The tour was hostile and lonely. But I miss the trips to Indonesia, boat trips to the Mentawais. I love the contest in Tahiti. I won four times. I loved going there just to surf perfect waves. I miss that sometimes."

After the Eddie, Keala wrote on Instagram, "This might be my last great #send—my body can't take this shit anymore. I hope you enjoyed the show."

But is retirement the next stop on the boundary-breaking, justice-seeking big-wave maven's path? "It's not surf season so right now there's nothing to chase," she mulls. "But will I feel different, will I feel motivated, when Pipe is firing? You'll have to ask me then."

*Robert "Wingnut" Weaver in 1995 on the North Shore, Oahu, Hawaii. Photo by Tom Servais*

# 8.

# ROBERT "WINGNUT" WEAVER

## By Holly Peterson

*"For fifteen years now, Wingnut and my family have surfed together on the East and West Coasts, from Montauk to San Jose, and in Nicaragua, Mexico, and the Maldives. Wingnut and our motley crew of friends and family will sit on the lineup, yes, waiting our turn, letting better and more local surfers go first. And when the time comes, Wingnut can push me into the wave, and I'm proud of how I pop up, bottom turn, and go down the line, even if every single surfer reading this is thinking, This chick is a kook."*

PREFERRING TO JUST "GLIDE AND SMILE" DOWN THE WAVE, rather than having to catch it, the very humorous bestselling author Holly Peterson describes her experience of learning to surf, her very particular style, and her travel adventures with pro surfer Robert "Wingnut" Weaver, the longboarding star of *The Endless Summer II*. But Peterson also shares how surfing became her solace during the summer of 2006, "a year that left me drenched in a deluge of grief," she writes.

# CRY AN OCEAN

**Knuck·le·head**

/'nəkəl (h)ed/

**Noun:** *A term used to describe a person who exhibits inane and foolish behavior; often associated with longboarder Robert Weaver, commonly known as "Wingnut."*

Wingnut and I have a balanced relationship; call it mutual disrespect. I marvel at his inability to grow up; he mocks my surfing strategy. His disdain flows deep, no equivocating: "You're the only person I've ever met who has chosen a complete and literal hands-off approach to catching great waves," he tells me. "You have no interest in learning when to take off and when to paddle slowly or quickly."

"Your point being?" I get that my unusual approach to the sport annoys Wingnut. I enjoy annoying Wingnut.

"Other people like taking the challenge of nailing your timing." More of his pathetic Hail Marys. "They seek the grace of spinning around at the wave's peak, then digging your way in." For the record, I could not locate the peakish sweet spot of a wave if you were to offer me a 1967 mint-condition Porsche 911 for doing so.

So what if I view surfing as a team sport rather than a solo sport? I am an urban woman who started surfing at age forty-two, and the primary parent to Chloe, Jack, and Eliza. I have to surf safely. I write during the wee hours of the early, dark mornings as a journalist and an author, so when I carve out essential time with Wingnut on the ocean, I maximize pleasure over pain.

Our unconventional system is this: out on the lineup, Wingnut paddles up next to me, grabs the tail of my board, situates me at that elusive peak, and yells, "Dig, dig, dig like hell!" Or he'll motion for me to haul ass twenty yards over near him, because he's spotted a set rolling in from far off. He's always hunting for me, stretching his neck up like a stork, shielding the sun from his eyes, and squinting at the horizon. I cannot fathom how any human can gauge from two hundred yards away how the hell a wave will break once upon us. Sometimes I'll test myself and say, "That one looks good, right? One's coming out there, right?" He barely answers—a waste of his breath. I should know at this point that all waves look big and scary far off; few are ridable when they approach.

Wingnut pretends he doesn't give me a break for anything, but that sparkle in his eye telegraphs that he does—in the most empathetic and sincere manner. For the record, I'm not scared of the waves. I respect them. There's a difference. And a massive part of that respect comes from the life lessons Wingnut has taught me in the ocean.

"If a wave doesn't scare you, you can't catch it," he tells me. "It's got to be big enough to have some momentum to push you along the way." Wingnut figures it's his duty to wedge instructive pointers into my brick wall of a brain. "You should feel the terror of turning around in front of a giant avalanche of water. Any surfer knows you gotta face the wave, take its power and height, man up—pardon the expression—spin around, and go."

I respond, "Actually, I don't. You can do all that, and then I get to glide and smile."

Wingnut and I first met when I was splitting from my husband. My divorced friend Electra described the experience of every slow ticking second over the years of our breakup as *"brutale."* Powering through a demanding career didn't quell the sadness and agony, so it took a lot of sweaty tap-dancing on my part to keep my eleven-year-old, nine-year-old, and six-year-old on track.

Wingnut was one of the two stars of *The Endless Summer II*, which came out in 1994. Now, with his professional longboard career behind him, he oversees surf events and travels with families and friends as an instructor for all ages and mentor to the younger set. I introduced myself to him on a call out of the blue and asked if he'd meet us in Mexico. He did, and that's when our bizarre partnership blossomed. That's also when I discovered that surfing was my salve.

During this period of time, a lot of bad, life-altering stuff started to happen, which I'll explain in due time. I had a lot on my plate. We all have a lot on our plates. But this was an extra helping of sorrow and misery that no one ever wants to land on theirs.

My three kids and I started surfing over fifteen years ago—before I met Wingnut—at a surf camp on New York's Long Island. Kids are the best surf companions, because they are stupid fearless. One day in 2006, while I was jogging in the haze of an impossibly humid August, surfers teaching kids in the Atlantic caught my attention. I could hear them laughing from fifty yards away. I made a mental note to give my ten-year-old, Chloe, a surf lesson with a daughter of French friends staying for a month. The next day, when the instructors took the very game, very young girls much farther out than I felt comfortable with, I grabbed a foam board and jumped in, Mama Bear style, and paddled after them. Every parent knows the unique terror of something happening to someone's kid on our watch.

This may shock you, but my paddling technique was not sound at first. Of course, in an attempt to reach the girls, I did the basic surfer no-no of holding the board horizontally in front of my torso, so the crashing waves slammed me down, board on top. When I did manage to get on the board beyond the shore break, I failed to progress amid the swirling currents. A kind instructor named Java rescued me, pointed my board out to sea, and held it solidly in one spot as waves crashed on my head. Java is shaped like King Kong and can manhandle any wave for any client. He's known as one of the best surfers on the East End of Long Island. Wingnut pushes my board artfully, but Java's push is turbocharged: with his torque launching you, you could surf fifty yards on a flat lake.

That summer day, Java paddled me out by lumbering up on top of me and sped us out to the girls. With kids and instructors goofing it up, his dreadlocked friend Sunshine took a moment to help me catch my first wave. Suffice it to say, with his angling my board on the gentle swell, I sort of, kind of, stood up. I had the shocked expression of a kid riding a bike without training wheels for the first time. That one-millisecond nirvana of vertical gliding (walking on water, really) put dizzying swirls in my eyes.

My all-time happiest parenting moments include the times my kids, their friends, and I paddled like mad to drop into the same wave. As the sun set, we'd pile all salty and spent into my jeep parked in the sand and pass the evening hours arguing over who'd gotten the wave of the day. We've devised a strict point system: one point for each wave caught, five bonus points for the best trick of the day (say, best 360 twirl), and five bonus points for the biggest wave of the day. I'd always get as heated as my eleven-year-old about our wave-tally competitions. Our family friend Benji devised a two-point penalty for any time I got a push on a wave, and rightly so—it *is* unfair. With an instructor helping position me, I can get many more waves than they can, so it evens out to a close race. I most often deserve "wave of the day" if I may say so. I remind them to this day of that bomb I caught in Punta Mita, though our friends Jack and Teddy still won't admit it was the biggest wave of the session.

That "stoke" of surfing, as we call it, hooked me so profoundly that I'd spend late December afternoons those first few years in forty-five-degree water off the Beach 87 jetty at New York's Rockaway Beach. Under the roar of the afternoon 747s from Europe landing at JFK, we'd surf until the winter sideways light turned the water inky black. The lights of New York's skyscrapers twinkled in the dusk. At this point in the story, it should be clear to you that changing into a pee-smelling 6mm wet suit on dirty cement does not fit my usual persona of seeking the dirtiest martini in the highest heels or the most luxurious blowout.

Winter 5.4mm suits have a hood with a tight circular cutout, which scrunches my eyebrow to my bottom lip. I couldn't even put on the inflexibly thick rubber booties and gloves without a guy helping me. In Rockaway, I'd surf with generations of blue-collar Irish Catholic cops and firefighters who were relentless about getting their waves. Even though Java or Sunshine would meet me there so I could surf smart and safe, I once dropped in on a territorial surfer that first winter. He managed to avoid me and still surf gracefully down the line. Nonetheless, my transgression caused the local guy to scream, "Motherfucker!" I, the only mom out there at sundown, yelled back, *"Who the hell raised you?"*

For fifteen years now, Wingnut and my family have surfed together on the East and West Coasts, from Montauk to San Jose, and in Nicaragua, Mexico, and the Maldives. Wingnut and our motley crew of friends and family will sit on the lineup, yes, waiting our turn, letting better and more local surfers go first. And when the time comes, Wingnut can push me into the wave, and I'm proud of how I pop up, bottom turn, and go down the line, even if every single surfer reading this is thinking, *This chick is a kook.*

After a good wave ridden to shore, when I've battled the overpowering whitewater back out to the lineup to my limit, Wingnut has been known to go in and rescue me. How does he know that my point of pride has been breached, that my arms are overdone spaghetti noodles? When I do what any New Yorker would do. I raise my arm in the air and yell, "Taxi!" He powers in only when I have suffered for at least fifteen minutes; he is stern and stubborn about that. When he flies in to help me, catching any wave instantly anywhere near him, I grab his ankle, and he motors me back to the lineup like a human jet ski.

Despite his ruthless teasing, he does know I'm honestly trying my best in pretty big, macking sets. For this book, when I asked him his opinions about how we surf together, he conceded, "Like any action sport, if you're going to succeed at it when you decide to go, you have to fucking go. You are very good about that; I will give you that. You don't have any doubt when it's time to pull the trigger. I've seen so many people who think about it three times and hesitate. By the time they launch to their feet, they go over the handlebars, because the wave gets too steep. If you can charge at the right time, you'll make ninety percent of the waves, and you do that very, very well."

That's the first nice thing Wingnut has ever said about me, and I'll take it. And I'm putting it in print right here.

What exactly is it about the church of surfing that gives all its disciples—from famous pros to Venice Beach surf rats to corporate titans—that stoke, the same mesmerized spirals in their eyes? It's different from other sports in that the currents, underwater wipeouts, and shifting surface conditions require three-dimensional concentration. Whether you're carving figure eights on fresh backcountry powder, hammering that drive straight down the middle of the fairway, or riding a bike down a hill for the first time in second grade, consider that thrill you feel down to your toenails, then cube it. That's where surfing takes you, even when it pummels you.

Unlike most other sports, surfing gives you no stable ground beneath your feet—no semipredictable, immobile ski slope or mountain bike path on which you can rest to assess the steepness. Once you go over the edge and commit to riding a wave, there's no going back. Surfing is a constant, no-frills metaphor for life: peering off the peak of that big-ass wave, readying your triceps to push you from your stomach to your feet, you feel in your veins that now or never, you have to charge. There is a brief moment of suspension out in thin air where you visualize the consequences of your choice. You have precisely a millisecond of decision time; after that, if you hesitate, gravity will pull that nose down, and the propulsion of the wave will flip the tail up and over. If you commit, your toes grab the bumpy, skidproof wax, and you swing your weight into a beautiful bottom turn before you tear down the line.

Even the best surfers find themselves under several feet of pummeling whitewater when a barreling wave suddenly envelops them from above, below, and all sides. Under nature's pressure, you can't even figure out which way is up. With an epic wipeout, the seconds tick differently, as if relativity actually slows time down under crushing water—another ultimate metaphor for the value of patience over panic.

And panic you must not: rushing to an abstract surface induces sprinting heartbeats, which deplete oxygen. You have to relax mentally and slow your heart, just like one of those crazy people who deep-dive without oxygen.

Though this may sound counterintuitive, that's my favorite part of surfing: getting pounded and held down by a terrifying monster wave.

Managing my reaction under crushing water relies on equal parts yin and yang, submission and power. All at once, I'm in peaceful submission to a force greater than me and possess the power to battle fear and slow my heart in its split second of need. This harmonious release and control place me into a Buddhist-monk-level nirvana, so much so that I cry joyful tears when I come up for air.

I'm hoping he won't read this part, but Wingnut is one of the greatest longboarders ever. He doesn't even remember how he got his nickname. It was in his teens, "and it just stuck," he told me in that surfer way of ignoring things in life most people fixate on. Surfers embody a unique ability to weed out the bullshit in life, which allows us to know what about life is worth digging in for and when.

"I grew up on a swim team and knew how to body surf. So, it was just adding the complication of a surfboard to the adventure," he explains. He started surfing at age seventeen just north of Newport pier at Blackies beach. "Watching all these guys every morning, I do remember a fascination with their skill level. One guy, Don, was the best nose rider, and Kenny had the best bottom turn. Someone else was the best goofy foot I've ever seen. I just wanted to surf with each of those guys as much as possible. I wanted to get much better than them. It probably took me at least six months to learn—well, become a competent surfer enough for them to give me shit."

*Robert "Wingnut" Weaver in 1996 on the North Shore, Oahu, Hawaii. Photo by Tom Servais*

At this point in time, in his late teens, he was sleeping in a single bed in his "shitty" studio. "I had a curtain that was a dark sheet with thumbtacks—back then, I didn't have any fucking money to buy anything."

In 1991, he married Janice Barr, an angel who let him surf all day. That turned out to be a good relationship tactic with a surfer, because just a year into their marriage, Wingnut got a call from Hollywood. Director Bruce Brown called him about starring in *The Endless Summer II*. Wingnut had just graduated from the University of California San Diego with a degree in economics. (Yes, one can be highly intelligent and still be a knucklehead. Some of the biggest knuckleheads are the smartest people I know. Authentic smart-aleck, wise-cracking talent has witty bait-and-switch at its core.) The filming took eighteen months, but he got to do what every surfer dreams about: surf Jeffreys Bay in South Africa to Ollie's Point in Central America with Laird Hamilton, Gerry Lopez, and Shaun Tomson. Many others of equal talent could have played the part, but Wingnut is a high-level hambone and was perfect for the role.

My friend Dave Sokolin, who owns a family wine business in Manhattan, has also traveled the globe on boys' trips with Wingnut on the *Four Seasons Explorer*, a surfing catamaran with sixteen cabins. "Wingnut brings more aloha to the sport than anyone I've ever met," Dave explains. "He'll also moon you as he's surfing by, most likely in a handstand."

Wingnut surfs like a Harlem Globetrotter plays ball, but he's there to keep us prudently aware of the power of the ocean. Wingnut feels in his bones where the six kids are in our pack, which is not easy on huge waves in a foreign land that are constantly changing. Wind spray, intense sun glare, and high crashing whitewater mean I always lose sight of them, which definitely makes my heart race. "First off, I'd take a bullet or shark bite for any family that entrusted me in the ocean," he tells me. "But mostly, I know when the surf is too big or shallow, or my clients are too tired to be safe. They have to push it, but not where the risk outweighs the rewards."

I've only cried once from a wipeout, while surfing in Indonesia. Going over the falls means being in the wrong place at the wrong time, that you've failed to paddle away from or over a colossal wave—defying gravity as it sucks up water *and you* in its curling centrifugal power. You get pounded back onto the water as if a giant pro wrestler has slammed you down, your board on a rubber band, ten-foot leash snapping back and banging you as you somersault.

I went over the falls on a giant Bali set wave I shouldn't have been near, couldn't paddle hard enough from the impact zone to clear. Once out and alive, I lay on my stomach, rested my head on my hands, and convulsed. For a really long time. And then I thought, "Fuck this sport. What the fuck am I doing on a way-too-big Indonesian big-boy break?" Let it be known that Wingnut was not with me on that trip, he reminds me. And I got onto the boat and went back to my room. Yes, I returned the next day, but on baby waves. I was quiet and shook for days.

However, amid these joyous, sometimes petrifying waves, a deeper undertow was tugging at my story. Surfing became a solace during the summer of 2006, a period in my life that left me drenched in a deluge of grief. During that time, four of my favorite men, the luminous threads in the fabric of my life, left this world: Anthony, Judd, Neil, and Artyem. Their abrupt departures left a void; the saltwater of my tears from that time could fill an ocean. And another again.

Of the men I lost, all were my best friends; maybe one was a lover. OK, maybe two, but don't tell anyone. I worked with them during my years at ABC News, pulling punch-drunk all-nighters on overseas trips and partying hard with them at home. There was Anthony, the prankster and prince; Judd, the charmer and goofball; Neil, the protector who shielded us from the world's adversities; and Artyem, the fearless Russian renegade whose voice against the Soviet status quo echoed far and wide. With these boys lost forever, the ground crumbled beneath me. They were my rocks, and now everything felt rocky.

So, what else does a New York working mother do when her four favorite boys on the planet die? I surfed—every day, everywhere. On flat days, I'd paddle around like a platypus just to feel the water I propelled, the rigid board swaying under my torso. One day in Mexico, dirt from the highway had rinsed out a hundred yards into the sea after heavy rains. The waves were a big, mushy mess, the grayish-blue water storming on the horizon and tan, muddy water in a vast hundred-yard-wide triangular shape right in the break. No one dared go in. But I did. I remember my friends and family eating tacos on the deck and shaking their heads at me. *What is up with her?*

What was up with me was this: I needed rinsing out from my sadness, even in filthy highway runoff. I craved the comfort of saltwater that oozed around me like amniotic gel.

Wingnut's immature, idiotic *knucklehead* humor became a tether to joy amidst a storm of my dying men. His constant teasing was a reminder of Anthony's practical jokes, of Judd's bad-boy belly laughs, of Neil's selflessness in war zone safety for others, of Artyem's unfathomable courage in resisting authoritarian power. For every jibe Wingnut throws at me, there is a lesson; for every (earned and valid) criticism of my style and please-push-my-ass-in strategy, a comforting rub on the back.

Amidst and after all the death and divorce hell, Wingnut and I adventured to the Maldives with my oldest daughter and three other eighth-grade boys. From midnight to dawn, our steady catamaran with twelve cabins tore through the black and sometimes angry sea, hopping from island to island in search of the best arrangement of wind and swell.

Dreamlike clear waves come in rhythmic stripes over the Maldives, an archipelago and the planet's lowest country (at four feet above sea level). From the expanse of the Indian Ocean, which reaches twenty-six thousand feet in depth, those azure lines broke against the shallow reef beneath us, forming curlicues of see-through perfection. We'd race down the line, the whitewater roaring after us like a pack of wild dogs. A few men stood guard on a small Zodiac closer to shore in case a quick rescue was in order. One day, I ungracefully flopped my body over the boat's rubber edge after one of my particularly epic, starfish-shaped wipeouts. The Maldivian on board added this gracious comment: "No offense, laaydy, but your daughtah surfs much bettah than you."

Wingnut, always caring and generous to me, focused on the kids during the first few days or the trip; then he wanted to help me get my best-ever wave. The night before, he told the kids they weren't surfing until he said so. When they started to complain, he gave them a look that signaled, *"I'll ground you on the boat for a day if you can't respect that it's your mom's time to shine."* Wingnut and I alone went out in the darkness before dawn while the boatmen were sleeping, so we had the Farm break to ourselves as a rising fireball illuminated the water.

"You remember that enormous one in the Maldives," he still says years later over a beer.

"Always will," I reply.

On those very same waves where legends surf, our gang tried our hardest to ride in that sweet middle spot of each wave from sunrise until the moon shone. It would take ten minutes to scrub the sunscreen and salt off our bodies, and each night, I did so alone in the outdoor shower hose off the boat's back-stern sea-level ledge. One evening, I slipped on the sudsy shampoo and almost fell into the inky black currents that would have taken me out to the endless expanse of the Indian Ocean before anyone knew I was gone.

That night, that near-fatal slip, haunts me to this day and proves chances are greater I could die in the shower well before a great white takes a chomp out of my torso.

I still mourn Anthony never learning to surf, that we, in our twenties and thirties together, always on beaches, never even considered trying it. We always fueled each other's nonsense, upping the ante to our antics. He'd challenge me with a dare, electricity in his eyes recharged and rerouted back to him by mine. Another reason to try something stupid, another opportunity to laugh. Our special brand of fun (which no one else understood) would be ours forever. Forever feels believable with a friend. It's forever until it isn't.

We worked together at ABC News, and we spent our summer Saturday nights with other network news pals doing "slammers," some idiotic drinking game from my high school that I taught them. We'd bang a coffee mug filled with half ginger ale and half vodka on the table, which would cause it to bubble up, which meant we could take about four shots down in a few gulps.

Coming from a fancy family in Europe, Anthony wore beautiful cashmere and custom shirts while everyone else in the office wore wrinkled button-downs and running shoes. Our shared office space was less a workspace and more a cauldron of mischief and mirth. But all those lighthearted moments were juxtaposed with his struggle against cancer, which he battled with the purest form of grace.

To put cancer in the back of his mind, Anthony distracted himself with planning the next practical joke, often on our esteemed boss, Diane Sawyer. Once, Anthony pretended he was Princess Caroline's aide-de-camp in the principality of Monaco, calling Diane out of the blue.... At the time, every news anchor desperately wanted an interview, or "get" as TV people say, with Princess Caroline. This supposed aide-de-camp scolded Diane in a heavy French accent from the minute she picked up the phone. She wasn't addressing him properly as "Monsieur le Générale." She flogged herself verbally to save the day, eventually winning him over with enough entreaties to secure the interview's date, time, and conditions. And then Anthony cracked up, and Diane marched down the office hall, arms pumping, to murder him.

When I was trying to change jobs, to no avail, Anthony pretended he was CBS News trying to poach me from ABC News. My phone rang. "This is CBS News President Andrew Heyward. We're looking for new PAs and hear you're really good." I should have remembered that news presidents don't offer lowly production assistants jobs; HR people beneath them handle this.

I was so confounded I was unable to speak. Could it be that someone, a news division president no less, understood what a great production assistant I was? He said it again: "You're good, really good."

Silence again. And then I added, suppressing a self-assured smile, "Well, Andrew, yeah, I know. I am good. I am really kind of good." Silence again. And then Anthony started laughing, and I too felt positively homicidal. Of course, he then ran around and told everyone in the office what a conceited, gullible schmuck I was.

Anthony died of cancer hours after he left my family home, after a terrible battle over years. I remember once sitting on a friend's deck in front of the ocean with him in the last few weeks of his life; he was a mere skeleton of his former self. I had just run over the seagrass dune with my soaked two-year-old. At this point, he couldn't get out of his chair without a heavy lift from under his armpits by a strong man. He said, "I'll never run over a dune like that again."

Phrases those spectacular men uttered during those sad years come back to me to this day. At lunch, through moist eyes, Judd, the news anchor, announced, "*This is going to be the last time I see you.*" A malignant brain tumor had invaded his brain, and his face was swollen from steroids. He looked like the sweetest, most earnest monster in a children's book. How does someone answer a statement like that without crumbling?

During this dark period of my life when "Only the Good Die Young" became my daily reality four times over, the saltwater felt like a womb. Wingnut became my anchor in the vast ocean, far more curative than a yoga class or even a good cry.

Neil died of a stroke after a month-long hospital stay. Running the overseas operations of ABC News, from Tehran to Moscow, he ensured that producers, camerapeople, and correspondents had money, battle helmets, cash, plane tickets, food, permissions, and visas. We'd smoke Marlboro Reds late at night, and dine on cucumbers and stale bread washed down with vodka. We marveled at the irony of a Soviet Ministry of Innovation when the United States broke the barriers of bureaucracy as the USSR fell. In that four-week post-stroke hospital stay, Neil didn't utter a word until the very end. The nurse had started to describe more unpleasant, useless interventions, and he murmured his first and only one word in those four weeks. "*Bullshit!*" he announced, and perished soon after.

*I'll never run over a dune like that again.*

*This is going to be the last time I see you.*

*Bullshit!*

Artyem didn't get to say any words I can recite because he didn't know he was going to die. The last time I saw him, he sat with me at his wife's bedside in New York's Mount Sinai Hospital after the birth of their second son. We drank warm champagne from Styrofoam cups. He was a renegade news anchor in the 1980s USSR who exposed the horrors of the Soviet invasion of Afghanistan. Those in power let him literally "air" his views due to his bravery and popularity. Bucking Soviet authority, he reported from the front and told the truth of atrocities to a public honed on Pravda propaganda. Ironically, when the Soviet Union liberalized and broke up into sixteen republics in the early 1990s, those in Moscow started to treat him differently—he had more authorities watching his movements with more scrutiny. And one day, his plane took off, and right off the runway it fell to the ground and blew up. There was an issue with the wing, they said. We don't know if it was a defective wing or if someone on the tarmac ensured it was a faulty wing.

Illness set in when Wingnut was too young as well. But he's been lucky, unlike my four favorite men who saw early ends. He's had multiple sclerosis for three decades and manages to surf and keep it under control. "Once my son was three, and then five, and then ten, I said to myself, *You know what?*" Wingnut told me. "*I will make it through this with him, getting to do things with him.* But then, at a certain point, he's just using all my wetsuits and leaving them wet in a pile, and I am now cursing the fact that my understanding was, the kid I always wanted to surf with was surfing more than me, and abusing all my shit."

These days, two decades later, a bath soothes me, but the ocean still cures me. I crave the sea before my eyes open on summer mornings when I am lucky enough to be near it. On empty early-morning sands, I run to the water and drench myself in the salt water; images of happy times in the surf fly by like cards in a circular, old-style Rolodex: contests and arguments over who got the "wave of the day," watching my kids glide on a board for the first time, shocked looks on their faces like little colts pushed up to stand by their mother's noses.

And so it is; memories of my lost men lead me to go back to the Maldives. One afternoon in the impossibly aquamarine sea, far in the distance, we see a wooden object bobbing in the ocean. A slight haze distorts the horizon of the break as I straddle my surfboard just before dusk. I can't measure the next set of waves until they are literally upon me, but visions of the eight-foot swell the day before are fresh in my mind. Fear is nothing but the stories we tell ourselves. This is my mantra as I wait for those corduroy rolls to arrive.

That wooden something-or-other confounds all of us in the lineup. Trying to place what it is, we are not scared of it; it's clearly inanimate. In the outer Maldivian atoll, what feels like ten thousand miles between our space and the next large chunk of land, the object gets nearer as currents pull it in.

I realize it's *a friggin' chair*: a bistro chair with red-and-white plastic woven strips peeling off it. Something you'd see in Paris at a sidewalk café. It's beat up, but it's solid. You could sit on it. Wingnut is stretching his stork neck to gauge the size and safety of the next set; he is, I realize then, our very own exceptional Orion, the celestial hunter.

I'm lying on my board, prepped for my team-engineered takeoffs. But the chair gets me thinking, and I sit up, restraddle the board, and consider the possibilities arising before us. "Wingnut, look at that chair; you know what you're doing with it, right?"

That sparkle crackles between us, just like mine and Anthony's did. No one else understands our particular brand of Mama Bear and Teacher Pro sparkle. "Of course, you idiot," Wingnut answers. "I know exactly what I'm doing with that chair."

I scream at the kids to watch the beautiful madness that is Wingnut. Of course, he then does what we pals, lucky enough to paddle in his midst, knew he would do. He powers out and grabs the chair, puts it upright on his board, and secures it with his chin firmly pressing on the bar between the legs. Chair stable, he now paddles over huge swells toward the incoming set. We lose him for a moment. He must have lost the chair; surely, he can't hold on to a ratty bistro chair in big sets while paddling. No one could do that for this long in this swell, right?

Next, the kids' chins have dropped to their boards, maybe to the bottom of the sea. Wingnut rides the wave toward us, sitting in his bistro chair atop the board. For extra credit, he has crossed his legs and pretends to take a sip of tea, his pinky facing the heavens, toasting those who once felt joy on Earth and those who still get to feel it now.

*Bethany Hamilton in 2017 on Kauai, Hawaii. Photo by Mike Coots*

# 9.

# BETHANY HAMILTON

## By Captain Brett Crozier, US Navy (Retired)

*"Over the years, I've been fortunate to meet many decorated combat veterans, and Bethany would have fit right in with these heroic men and women. You could trade a surfboard for a fighter jet, but the perseverance, courage, and success would remain the same."*

Retired US Navy Captain Brett Crozier, a surfer himself, writes about Bethany Hamilton, who was a rising surfing star in 2003 at thirteen years old when a shark attack in Kauai took her left arm. It was headline news around the world. Less than a month later—twenty-six days, to be exact—Hamilton was back in the ocean surfing. She entered her first major competition six weeks later, won her first national surfing title within two years, and turned pro by the age of seventeen.

Crozier made his own headline news years later in March 2020. Then the commanding officer of the USS *Theodore Roosevelt*, the most prestigious carrier in the US fleet, Crozier was dismissed for not following protocol after a letter was leaked alerting higher-ups that COVID-19 was spreading through his ship.

Though their age, professions, and personal journeys have followed drastically different paths, Crozier, a surfer and the author of *Surf When You Can: Lessons in Life, Loyalty, and Leadership from a Maverick Navy Captain*, shares how their passion for the ocean, families, and surfing unites them more than what sets them apart.

# BETHANY HAMILTON'S PERFECT DAY

A Navy career is an adventurous one. During my thirty years in service, from 1992 to 2022, I was lucky enough to chase pirates from a helicopter over the open ocean, land fighter jets moving at 150 miles per hour on a moving flight deck, fly dozens of combat missions, and captain a nuclear-powered aircraft carrier stretching more than a thousand feet in length, navigating it across the globe with a crew of over five thousand Sailors. Along the way I was also able to sail, fight, and fly alongside some of the strongest and most capable men and women who volunteered to serve their country.

And of course, I surfed whenever I could. While a Navy career generally keeps you on or near the water, bringing a surfboard with you on a space-limited ship can be challenging. If I was traveling in a single-seat fighter jet, it was impossible. So sometimes I had to sneak my board onto the ship and stash it in an overhead space out of the way so it wouldn't get dinged, and sometimes I just had to be willing to surf with whatever board was available to rent at the local beach. But for a novice and an eager surfer like me, there was always a way.

On most deployments, we were at sea for at least a month between port visits. That gave me plenty of time to research the next port, find a suitable break that fit my skills, determine the best way to get there, and then put together a crew of willing adventurers. Although we weren't always successful, due to changing schedules or weather, it was a great distraction during that month at sea as we dreamed of our next surfing safari stop in places like Hawaii, Guam, the Philippines, Vietnam, Thailand, and many other places. While after weeks underway many Sailors onboard a Navy ship want to get far away from the ocean, the pull of the sea remained strong for me, and I found the need to get right back to it—this time on a surfboard instead of a one-thousand-foot aircraft carrier.

Bethany Hamilton did not serve in the military, and likely didn't have to wait a month between surf sessions, but she is a warrior nonetheless and is also strongly drawn to the ocean. She's some twenty years my junior, but Bethany has been an inspiration to me and many others because of her grit and determination. She found a way to overcome obstacles both physical and emotional and make it back to what she loved. Over the years, I've been fortunate to meet many decorated combat veterans, and Bethany would have fit right in with these heroic men and women. You could trade a surfboard for a fighter jet, but the perseverance, courage, and success would remain the same.

Though our professional journeys have followed drastically different paths, our shared passion for the ocean, our families, and surfing unites us more than sets us apart. Even though I'll never come close to matching Bethany's exceptional skills on a surfboard, our idea of a perfect day involves surfing, family, and similar goals.

Bethany was a rising surfing star in 2003 when she made headline news around the world at only thirteen years old, and lost her left arm after being attacked by a fourteen-foot tiger shark while surfing out at Tunnels Beach in Kauai. By the time she was rushed to the nearest hospital, Bethany had lost more than 60 percent of her blood and was near death. To most casual observers, it seemed the attack would bring Bethany's childhood dreams to an unfortunate end. Sure, the sport had been a part of her life since she was a child, but I don't know many *adults* who would even consider getting back in the water after such an event, let alone a teenager. But as the world was about to learn, Bethany Hamilton is anything but typical.

"When you go through something as traumatic as I did, so much comes back to my mindset," Bethany once stated. "I was just thankful to be alive. Lying in the hospital after the attack and realizing my arm is gone, I knew my life was going to be very different. I thought my dreams were gone, and I didn't know what my future held." Mike Coots, a friend who had learned to surf again after losing his leg to a shark, visited Bethany in the hospital and inspired her that she could surf again if she wanted to. "All I needed was a hit of inspiration, and I was on a mission," she said.

Less than one month—twenty-six days, to be exact—after the attack, Bethany was back in the ocean, surfing on a longboard. While she did not know anyone who surfed with one arm, she was willing to try. She was willing to explore unknown territory.

Bethany entered her first major competition only six weeks later, won her first national surfing title within two years, and turned pro by the age of seventeen. It was a comeback that defied all the odds—physically, mentally, and emotionally. It would have been difficult enough to surf with the use of only one arm, but for that young girl, barely a teen, to have the strength of character and fearlessness that it took to get back on the board in the waters around Kauai…well, that's the stuff of legend.

Sure, I've long coveted Bethany's strength and deftness on a board, a skill level I know I could never hope to attain. But like most people who know her, I admire Bethany for her spirit as much as her surfing prowess. In fact, in the two decades that have passed since the attack, Bethany has touched the hearts and lives of countless others with her messages of faith, tenacity, and courage. Ironically, she has been able to reach far more people as a result of the attack than she would have from surfing alone. Devout Christian that she is, Bethany likely would say she was fated to walk this path in life, which she's done with grace, dignity, and fire.

As I delved deeper into Bethany's story, my research began to ignite a series of questions in my brain. Most of these were not about the younger Bethany, but rather about the Bethany Hamilton of today. No longer a professional surfer, though she surfs in the odd event here and there, she has been married for ten years to Adam Dirks and recently gave birth to the couple's fourth child. Now Bethany counts herself as a mother, wife, author, motivational speaker, and mentor. *What inspires her?* I asked myself. *How has what happened to her as a teen affected and molded her into the woman she is today? How does she balance life and work? What legacy does she hope to leave for her children?*

Yet as I pondered these questions, I found that I kept circling back to one principal notion over and over again, an idea that all of the others seemed to eventually lead to: I wanted to know how the thirty-three-year-old Bethany Hamilton of today would spend a perfect day. It's not as far-fetched a question as you might think; the ideal has long captured the imagination of the surfing community. In fact, in the very first issue of *SURFER* magazine, published back in 1962, the editorial sign-off spoke to that connection: "In this crowded world, the surfer can still seek and find the perfect day, the perfect wave, to be alone with the surf and his thoughts."

For me, asking Bethany that one simple yet profound question not only would give her the opportunity to examine her life on both a macro and micro level, but would also help answer (I hoped) everything else I wanted to know about her. Having been through what can only be described as a nightmare experience on a surfboard, would surfing be a part of her perfect day? Who would she spend it with? What would she choose and why? And most important, what would those choices say about how she views the world and her place in it?

Interestingly, the exercise also prompted me to consider the same question for myself. How would a retired Navy captain and former fighter pilot—one that had been through his own life-changing experience—craft *his* perfect day?

In March 2020 I was lucky enough to be the commanding officer of the USS *Theodore Roosevelt*, the most prestigious carrier in the US fleet. That's when COVID-19 spread through the ship like wildfire, leading me to take steps to protect the lives of the five thousand Sailors onboard. Ultimately it led to my dismissal, because my actions were perceived by the brass back at the Pentagon to have rocked the boat more than they should. The crew gave me a cheering send-off when I left the ship that could be rivaled only by a winning Super Bowl team at a hometown parade. I have no regrets or anger at how things unfolded, and I remained on active duty until 2022. If I wasn't willing to risk my career for the safety of my crew, then I wasn't qualified to lead them from the beginning. While the COVID pandemic proved to be a life-changing experience for me, I realize it was not nearly as significant as the one Bethany faced at a much younger age.

So thinking of my perfect day was a fun yet daunting exercise, and one that forced me to consider aspects of my life that I don't often dedicate a lot of thought to. And I realized that, as it was for Bethany, surfing remained an important way for me to continue to find balance and clarity—in my case, when my thirty-year career ended under the spotlight of world events.

Even though I started out believing that Bethany and I were vastly different, the opportunity to get to know more than just her headlines quickly taught me otherwise. We share many commonalities: themes of nature, simplicity, and family that seem to transcend geography, gender, and age and ultimately make us much more alike than we are different. And in a time when the world often seems balanced on a knife point of global crisis, it is a wonderful reminder that as humans, we are all connected on a level that too often we fail to recognize.

Like most parents who have just welcomed a new child into the world, Bethany begins her perfect day by opening her eyes and realizing that her entire brood has slept through the night without interruption. A full night's sleep is a rare gift for a mother of four children under the age of nine. But it doesn't take long before the house is astir with activity and Tobias (eight), Wesley (five), Micah (two), and Alaya (six months) are bouncing on their parents' bed.

Yet unlike so many of us—especially young parents—who stumble through our mornings without much thought or intention, Bethany takes a more considered approach to her day. She recognizes that the first few minutes after she wakes up can help set the tone for everything else that follows. So rather than let the day take her for a ride (this is her perfect day, after all), she chooses its course with both intention and purpose. It's this sort of mindful, proactive outlook that Bethany believes can help all of us lead more fulfilling lives, whether each day carries the flag of perfection or not. And the best part? It only takes a minute or two, she says.

I'm not particularly surprised that Bethany opts to begin her day this way. After all, this is still the same person who essentially walked out of the hospital and back into the ocean some twenty years ago after being bitten by a shark. Clearly she values the importance of mindset and attitude, and the role that those two things can play in health and well-being.

On Bethany's perfect day, she removes herself from the bustle of the family and finds a quiet place in the house to sit with her own thoughts while Adam minds the children. She begins her mental cleansing process by reading the Bible, an encouraging book, a thoughtful prayer to set the pace of the day and push aside any negative thoughts and stresses that may be forcing their way to the forefront of her consciousness.

Bethany refuses to let the memory of the shark attack define who she is. On the contrary, she consciously focuses on the many wonderful things that make up her extraordinary life. This kind of positive morning mindset routine pays dividends throughout the day by forcing us to look past the things that stand between us and happiness. In that way, we can all get back on our own surfboards and face our greatest fears.

Intentions now set, Bethany's perfect day sees her return to a kitchen abuzz with activity. Her children are fully engrossed and engaged in a healthy breakfast bursting with local foods and fruits; a bowl heaped with sautéed vegetables and eggs topped with avocado and goat cheese atop a slice of fresh sourdough toast is the focal point of this particular meal. Outside, the early-morning Hawaiian sunshine casts a golden glow across the grass; the day beckons with promise. *It does indeed seem perfect.*

Yet, as Bethany looks toward the ocean from her home on Kauai, she takes a moment to sit with the realization that she alone is not responsible for the bounty of her life. Once again, she anchors herself in something deeper than the here and now.

"I know that the life I've been given is a gift," she says. "Every day I'm inspired by my faith in God and by the beauty and challenge in the raw nature."

As Bethany and I sink deeper into our conversation, I can't help but notice that this is a woman who seems to be as comfortable in her own skin as anyone I've ever met. Sitting on a lanai outside her home, as the Pacific breeze occasionally tousles her blond hair, she seems at peace, happy.

"OK, now that breakfast is out of the way," I say, "what's next?"

I'm no journalist, so admittedly I have a vested interest in her answer. As an avid amateur surfer, I *want* the sport to play an integral role in her perfect day…but it's impossible to say whether it will. Maybe, like so many other professional athletes, she has come to view surfing more as a job than a passion and has grown tired of her work. Fair enough; there are so many other things out there to see and do, and Bethany strikes me as the kind of person who wants to see and do it all. But she does not disappoint. Like so many of us who discover the sport, surfing is woven into the very fabric of her life. It's not a job; it's probably not even a sport, per se. It's a connection with something bigger.

"I think of all of the pains and struggles that I've gone through, and really it's God that has gotten me through all that. But at the same time, God gave me this passion to surf, and it wasn't like that passion was taken too. My life could have looked a lot different after losing my arm. I could have lived a simple and quiet life, but I still wanted to surf."

*Courtesy of California Surf Museum, www.surfmuseum.org*

It was this connection that ultimately got Bethany back in the water all those years ago. Was she scared? Of course she was. But once she realized that the odds of a single shark attack were one in a million (let alone the odds of a second attack), she could not resist the draw of the ocean, even though she was only thirteen years old. As she says, her fear of losing surfing was greater than her fear of sharks. And so, her relationship with the water persists to this, her perfect day. Fed, motivated, and energized, Bethany heads to the beach. At first, though, it's just her and Adam, to catch what she calls "mom-and-dad" waves.

"Before we take the children out, we like to catch some proper surf," she says with a chuckle. "Those waves are a little bigger and a little heartier than the ones for the kids."

For now, anyway. Bethany says her oldest son, Tobias (age eight), is quickly growing into an accomplished surfer in his own right and can go down the line with the best of them. As for the younger ones, well, they're strictly limited to what Bethany calls "children's surf." And while Bethany has never related the story of the shark attack to her kids, the world is a very small place, and they've learned about it through other sources (older cousins, it seems, could not keep the tale to themselves). If this realization had any effect on her children's love of the water, though, it's certainly not evident by the way they throw themselves into the day's activities.

As for Bethany, the shark attack has never dampened her feelings about the water…or the creatures themselves. In fact, in the years since the attack, she actually took the time to swim with sharks herself, if only to come to peace with what had happened. So when the opportunity comes to surf—whether mom-and-dad waves or something a little tamer—she jumps all over it. Bethany is happy to simply be outside, whether it's in the water or on the beach, on her own board or playing in the break with her kids. And while she has embraced the many roles she now plays in the lives of her friends, family, and fans, simply being on the board can be a transcendent experience. As so many of us know, surfing is pushing the reset button on life.

"Being in nature is the obvious benefit—the sunshine and the calming beauty," she says. "But being away from the noise on land is just as important. Sure, you can bring it with you by keeping it in your thoughts, but those stresses all melt away when you're up and riding a wave, because you can't think about them. I love that aspect of surfing, of just being able to let go of your worries and your fears, your stresses and your challenges."

That's one thing that hasn't changed for Bethany. In the thirty-odd years she's been surfing, the ritual, the act, and the *feel* of the sport haven't changed at all for her. If anything, her decision to leave professional surfing behind has perhaps only allowed her to enjoy it more, not less.

"I'm definitely more relaxed about it now," she says. "When I was younger, I was always in a hurry to get my next wave, be the best in my sport. Now, I'm just excited to be in the water and am driven by something deeper than being the best. Now I push myself to be a great mom and take care of myself so I can keep doing what I love to do.

"Don't get me wrong; I'm still really competitive!" she adds quickly, laughing at her own omission. "But now I take the time to appreciate it more. And maybe that can't be taught. I mean, I think all my children will probably learn to surf, but I imagine one of them will probably love it more than the others."

As the saying goes, a bad day surfing is better than a good day at work.

"I'm happy to hear that surfing is such an important part of your perfect day," I say, breathing a sigh of relief. "But where on Kauai are you catching these waves? I mean, what's your favorite break?"

Bethany doesn't skip a beat. "Oh, there's no good surf here," she says, respecting the age-old surfing mantra of protecting your local break from invaders and tourists. "You have to go to Oahu for that. I hear the break at Waikiki is legendary!"

Fair enough; it was a silly question, and I should have known better than to expect Bethany to reveal such a closely guarded secret. Suffice it to say that she's *not* going to Waikiki for her perfect day. Given the opportunity, though, there are a couple of places outside of Hawaii that Bethany would jump at the chance to surf. One she's ridden before; the other is a lifelong dream.

"I think my favorite break in the world is probably the Macaronis in Indonesia," she says. "There's a barrel; there's ripping. It's super fun, but there's an intensity about it too, so it's the best balance. And you know when you're surfing it that waiting just around the corner can be that heavy-duty, fear-factor sort of wave."

If there's anything that speaks to the palpable difference between Bethany's surfing abilities and mine, that's it: she yearns for the intense break of a place like Macaronis, while I'm completely satisfied with long, slow breaks, like the one offered by the waters around my Southern California home. In fact, if I had to choose one break as my favorite, it would be White Plains Beach at Barbers Point, Hawaii. For it was in those family-friendly waters that I first learned to surf, where long days as a rookie Navy helicopter pilot were capped off with idyllic evenings in the most beautiful waters I'd ever known.

Bethany, on the other hand, has loftier expectations. For example, the one break that she yearns to ride is Skeleton Bay in Namibia, on Africa's southwest coast. Considered the world's longest sand-bottomed left-hand wave, it only came to fame in the early 2000s, thanks to legendary South African surfer Grant "Twiggy" Baker. This is definitely *not* a spot for children, as its impossibly long barrels churn out some of the fastest and thickest sand-dredging tubes on the planet.

"Those waves are insane!" Bethany exclaims, her competitive fire burning bright. "It's a professional, world-class wave. You take off super fast, and it's a really quick down-the-line, grindy sort of wave. I'd love to try it, though I say that with a healthy fear. I'd hate to fly all the way there and then not perform well. But if you do perform well, it can be the best ride of your life." It's hard to imagine Bethany ever thinking that she might *not* perform well on a board, but I guess that only goes to show that even the best among us have our occasional reservations and humility toward the ocean's raw power. The ocean seems to have a way of humbling even the best.

Of course, most of us are not surfing with only one arm. But if you think that's a deterrent, you don't know Bethany Hamilton. Of course, she didn't adapt immediately to the new set of physical circumstances that the attack had created for her, but it didn't take long. Bethany can paddle as fast and as straight with one arm as most people can with two, and when it comes to catching a wave, Bethany is a master of the late drop. Standing up on the board with the benefit of only one arm is also a challenge, but Bethany positions her right hand in the center of her board and uses the momentum of larger waves to help propel her upright. As for her boards, the only difference you'll notice is a small handle glued to the deck near the nose, which she uses for duck diving.

"Speaking of boards," I say, "you must have a favorite one that you're taking with you on your perfect day."

"Honestly, no," she replies. "In my experience, boards have a pretty short shelf life, so we're always on the hunt for the next best one. It's a strange paradox for a surfer: you're constantly saying goodbye to your favorite thing in the world…until you find the next one!"

But on her perfect day, Bethany is not leaving Kauai. Instead, she's enjoying the bulk of the day on the beach with her family. Whether she's surfing with Tobias and Wesley, splashing with Micah in the waves, or relaxing with Alaya on a blanket, it's a day grounded in the elemental forces of life that so many of us hold dear: family, nature, exercise, sunshine, love.

To help keep her children (and herself) focused on the here and the real and the now, electronic devices do not have a place in the story…not today, anyway. "Adam and I have made a conscious choice to keep the children off devices for as long as possible," Bethany says. But making the day device-free is as much about Bethany as it is about the kids. "There is no work on a perfect day!" she exclaims. "We're just living and enjoying what's in front of us.

"I think our world is so hyperconnected that it's so hard to turn it off sometimes," she adds. "And I feel that connectivity has changed our world so much. People are so addicted, and they don't even know it."

Maybe it's the mother in Bethany who has forged her beliefs about devices and connectivity. After all, she's very active on her social media accounts. But at the same time, she recognizes how devices can monopolize the attention of children and distract them from the beauty and adventure that surround them in the real world.

"I had this insane childhood—without devices—where my parents didn't know I was jumping off the rocks into the ocean, swimming with the turtles, and shell diving," she says. "But now you see the kids sitting on the rocks with their phones, *not* swimming with the turtles or diving for shells. It's an interesting transition."

"I think at the moment, people don't realize the detriment of it, but in ten years we'll hopefully start to find a better balance."

Chatting with Bethany not only gave me the opportunity to spend time with one of the legends of the sport, but also opened the door for me to reflect on my own life and the role that surfing has played in it. And while Bethany has competed at the highest levels and I, Brett Crozier, am 100 percent a recreational surfer, we both continue to appreciate the sport for what it offers the mind, body, and spirit. I guess that's why it's not surprising that surfing alongside my three boys with my wife, Mary, close by would be the foundation of my perfect day too.

More than that, though, spending time on the water has the uncanny ability to transport me back to my flying career, when my days were punctuated by a ritual and camaraderie matched by few pursuits…except surfing. I may be paddling the waters off Coronado Island, waiting for the next wave, but for a brief moment I'm a Navy fighter pilot once again, when a perfect day began with a morning flight on an F/A-18 over the Sierra Nevada mountains alongside a squadron of my closest friends and colleagues.

Like surfing, those missions—whether training exercises high above the beaches of Hawaii or active combat missions over Iraq—were a give-and-take of the exciting and the mundane, long minutes maintaining our formation punctuated by the adrenaline rush of dives, rolls, and dogfights. Afterward, we'd all get together in the briefing room to discuss the finer points of our mission, what went wrong and what went right—not unlike that group of friends who gather on the beach after a morning of surfing and compare notes on their triumphs and failures as they chow down on a pile of foil-wrapped breakfast burritos from a nearby joint.

Back on Kauai, Bethany's perfect day winds its way toward afternoon. She, Adam, and the kids are feeling satisfied and tired, that fulfilling kind of exhaustion that sets in when you've spent a day outside in the sun. Thankfully, it's *not* a feeling reserved for the surfers among us. Bikers, skiers, hikers…you name it. The process may not be the same, but the result is universal.

Tired but fulfilled, the family returns home, where the next order of events is a grand family barbecue. For this one, though, the guest list extends beyond the six of them. The barbecue is an extended-family affair: aunts, uncles, and cousins are there; the children spend time with Grandpa and Grandma, Bethany's parents. For Bethany and her children, this kind of get-together is not the stuff of fantasy, though, as her parents live in a guest house on her property.

"We have a good little tribe here," she says. "My parents have twelve grandchildren now, and we're all within striking distance of each other. We're pretty interconnected."

It's a joyous sight, here on the idyllic island of Kauai, arguably one of the most beautiful places on Earth. The adults sit and chat at a long family table set out on the grass; children are running, playing, and laughing. To the west, the sun sinks lower in the sky, soon turning into a red-orange ball glowing low on the horizon. A bonfire is definitely in the works, but for the moment, Bethany is lost in thought as she reflects on her day and her life, and how fortunate she's been to be able to turn what some people may view as a horrific experience into a message of hope and perseverance. She knows just how much of an inspiration she is to millions of people around the world, and the responsibility that comes with that fact is not lost on her. And yet, Bethany seems to handle it all with ease and grace.

"I grew up in a Christian home, and so much of my influence is to love others," she says. "I feel like I've already put much of my legacy out there, and I think my story really set me up to do that, to inspire and encourage other people, and to remind them that they can keep going when tough times come their way, even when they feel like they can't or the world around them doesn't think they can either.

"But not like in a fairy tale sense," she adds quickly. "This is more about real life, the gritty moments when no one's watching and you don't feel like paddling back out, but you keep pushing and pushing through those pain points when a lot of people would turn around and just kind of give up.

"So much of my life has been just believing that I can overcome whatever challenges have been put in front of me, and pushing myself to not let go of my God-given talents and skills."

If anything sums up Bethany Hamilton, that's it. An ocean of innate talent, strong religious beliefs, and enough warrior grit to keep going in the toughest of times. But more than that, Bethany is a person who has grown to appreciate everything that she has. It's a message she hopes to spread far and wide.

"I really love my life," she muses warmly. "And I look forward to it, which I think is rare for a lot of people. I don't like that the world has turned into that, but if we can find a way to still live our life, be a positive impact on those around us, and make the most of what we've got in every moment, then I think every day would be perfect."

*Michael February in 2020 at Jeffreys Bay, South Africa. Photo by Alan van Gysen*

# 10.

## MICHAEL FEBRUARY

### By Selema Masekela

*"I scoured all the pages of all the surf publications I could get my hands on in those days. I read the glossy periodicals cover to cover and studied every editorial photo, every ad. They all had one thing in sharp, unique common: none of the surfers in those pages, doing the thing I loved more than anything else, looked like me. They did not have an '80s high-top fade. None of them were Black. I can't begin to imagine what my late-teenage life, my young adult life, the entirety of my surfing existence would have looked like if a Black Michael February—one of the most gifted and innately stylish surfers that has ever roamed this green-and-blue planet—had existed when I started surfing."*

TELEVISION SPORTS COMMENTATOR, JOURNALIST, PRODUCER, AND MUSICIAN Selema Masekela writes about South African surfing sensation Michael February, whose presence on the world stage of professional surfing would not have been possible before the end of apartheid. Masekela, himself of South African descent, portrays how "the most racist and oppressive legalized system of governance" kept the majority of South Africa's beaches—including the famed Jeffreys Bay, considered one of the greatest surf breaks in the world—reserved for "Whites Only," and deprived the sport of both the unfathomable talent and the cultural influence that is Michael February.

# FEBRUARY

If you don't know who Michael February is, then watching him behind the scenes in the hours before his first heat at the 2023 Vans Pipe Masters, you might have a hard time being convinced that he was an actual competitor. On land he seems to be a quiet, almost outside observer of the spectacle that goes along with a competition of this immense stature. A calm so out of place that it could easily be confused for indifference. It doesn't quite go with the circumstances. This is Pipeline, one of the most intimidating, history-making waves on Earth. While his fellow competitors—the best in the world—are psyching themselves up, engaging in plyometric drills, hyperfocused on the ever-changing lineup, Mikey appears almost too chill. He engages in occasional light conversation, casually chases his young son around the competitors' area, and lounges with his wife, Zelti. High school sweethearts.

As his heat draws closer, he slowly makes his way to the area where his boards are stored and selects a craft to ride. He surveys and assesses a couple of the boards with his hands, slowly feeling down the rails, rubbing each board's belly on the underside, feeling for its weight under his arm. You can see him doing the math in his head as to how the board might play in the water relative to the conditions observed. Choice made, he deliberately changes into

his trunks, grabs his vehicle, kisses his son and wife, and nonchalantly walks his regal, six-foot-three-inch frame down a short set of stone stairs that will deposit him onto the deep, granular sand, that will deposit him into the violent beauty that is Pipeline.

As a brand-new, transplanted from the East Coast, and wholly obsessed seventeen-year-old surfer in the year of 1988, the walls of my bedroom were plastered with photographs of professional surfing in captured motion. I would stare at those photos for hours on end in both awe and wonder, daydreaming about what it might be like to tube-ride like Ronnie Burns, hack a powerful turn under the lip like Tom Carroll or Sunny Garcia, or sit in perceived oneness with the wave in the manner of Tom Curren. This was just a sampling of the many pro surfers I'd quickly come to idolize and aspired to be like. I carried these images in my head as references every time I paddled out at Cherry Street, my local break in Carlsbad, California. I desperately wanted to be in those pictures.

I scoured all the pages of all the surf publications I could get my hands on in those days. I read the glossy periodicals cover to cover and studied every editorial photo, every ad. They all had one thing in sharp, unique common: none of the surfers in those pages, doing the thing I had so quickly come to love more than anything else, looked like me. They did not have an '80s high-top fade. None of them were Black. I can't begin to imagine what my late-teenage life, my young adult life, the entirety of my surfing existence would have looked like if a Black Michael February—one of the most gifted and innately stylish surfers that has ever roamed this green-and-blue planet—had existed when I started surfing.

The absence of a Michael February on the world stage of professional surfing during the 1980s, 1990s, 2000s, and a majority of the 2010s is not an accident. It took place by exquisite design. When imagining the most racist and oppressive legalized system of governance they could, South Africa's apartheid architects likely weren't thinking about its long-term global effects on surfing. However, they didn't need to. Apartheid was essentially a one-size-fits-all Death Star of law after law after law that expertly dehumanized and severely restricted the movement of all nonwhite peoples within South Africa's borders. And like the Death Star, until it was ultimately destroyed in 1994, it perversely affected everything it touched. Picture American segregation and Jim Crow on performance-enhancing drugs. The truest evil. Besides regulating where Black South Africans could live and work, their property ownership, how they were educated, how they could think, who they could love, and so much more, apartheid had one particularly insidious superpower: restriction of movement. Movement to and from one's home could be questioned at any and all times. There needed to be a justifiable reason for wherever one would find themselves, provable upon request by the presentation of a passbook—essentially a passport with stamped receipts of all comings and goings.

Outdoor areas of potential recreation were especially reserved for the joy of white folks. And yes, you guessed it, that was especially the case for the ocean, with the majority of South Africa's beautiful beaches—especially the ones with the protective shark nets—reserved for Whites Only. What this means is that South Africa, a country with what is recognized as the greatest right-hand point break in the world, Jeffreys Bay, and world-class surf of all shapes and sizes up and down both its extended coasts, deprived itself of—and by default, cheated surfing as a whole out of—an unfathomable amount of world-class talent and cultural influence. I do not say this ignoring the indelible contribution of the man many call the blueprint of the modern-day professional surfer, one of the most influential surfers who has ever lived: 1977 world champion Shaun Tomson. Shaun put South African surfing on the global map. However, it is impossible to believe that Tomson's celebrated journey would've been remotely the same had it taken place in an apartheid-free professional surfing landscape.

Inevitably, though, while it's downright criminal that the world had to wait as long as it did for Michael February to come through and unintentionally yet wholly disrupt surfing, the universe found a way to right itself. Call it divine timing of the ancestors that the institutional portion of racism in South Africa structurally ended in 1994, and that, in anticipation of its ending, Michael February was born in Capetown, South Africa, on May 17, 1993.

To watch Michael February ride a surfboard is to watch an unrestricted free agent of artistic movement in motion. His surfing emits a frequency of sideways stance expression so unique, it simply cannot be ignored. It is musical. It is irreverent on the level of Miles Davis and John Coltrane, coupled with the unpredictable and infinite freestyle verse of Black Thought. It is Bad Brains, so you can't put in a box. The syncopation is distinctly South African, like township jive deep-fried in Amapiano. It is surfing so good, you can close your eyes and dance to it. Mikey allows himself to dance too long in the high line of a cylindrical eight-footer, flamboyantly accenting the high stakes with a split-second cross-stepped soul arch, only to instantly contract his long, languid physique impossibly low to his board, assuredly grabbing his outside rail with intention, to initiate a driving, torque-filled, downward carve with an arc so precise, an F1 driver who'd never seen surfing before in his life could only applaud.

Michael February's style is bathed in curiosity, possibility, and aquatic fun. Unlike the majority of his professional surfing peers in their prime, Mikey is not married to the high-performance thruster as his main mode of transport. I once went to a Neil Young show where he performed by himself, with no backup band. The stage was filled with every type of guitar, piano, keyboard, and organ you could imagine. Young casually strolled from instrument to instrument, storytelling in between, before settling on, say, a pipe organ, from which he'd perform a song you were surely familiar with, in a now beautifully unfamiliar way.

That is how February plays with surfboards—short twin fins, mid-length singles, and mid-length twins. He is as adept on an asymmetrical spacecraft as he is on a modern thruster. Mikey is capable of riding the same wave, on each craft, in a classic yet thoroughly unfamiliar and entertaining way. And perhaps the best part is that he never looks perfect doing so. He is not trying. His is a dance of visible micro-adjustments he does not try to hide, as he coaxes each unique craft into helping him discover new lines of infinite code, hidden in each and every wave.

I was in Johannesburg, South Africa, caring for my father, who was dying of prostate cancer, when I found out that Michael February had made it to the big leagues and qualified for a coveted spot on the upcoming 2018 World Surf League Championship Tour. In a 2012 interview, a writer for *The Inertia* asked me what it would be like to see a Black surfer one day make the tour. I responded that I hoped I'd get to see it in my lifetime, because it would mean so much that I would probably cry on that day. And now here I was having that moment, as I sat with my ailing father—who, despite thirty years of political exile, had fought with everything he had to see the machinations of apartheid end in his lifetime and return home to the country he loved with every fiber of his being. My father, his fellow political exiles, and the thousands of South Africans who sacrificed their lives in the fight to end apartheid couldn't have known they'd one day affect global professional surfing, yet here we were. The day had come.

*Michael February in 2020 at Scottburgh, Kwa-Zulu Natal Coast, South Africa. Photo by Alan van Gysen*

I told my father Mikey's story and showed him clips of his surfing. He smiled proudly and grooved with it. I use the term "grooved" because my father happened to be a musician by the name of Hugh Masekela, and to him, life was about repeatedly finding and sitting in the groove—that place where one creates or expresses themself from the deepest recesses of their being. The cellular truth space. There is no need to think when you are in the groove; you simply need to be all of what you have to give in that moment. Full stop. Discovering the trumpet as a teenager in the 1950s altered his existence. He began to relentlessly chase the groove. As a nineteen-year-old in 1960, chasing the groove helped him narrowly escape South Africa and live out his jazz dreams in New York City and the world. For the entirety of the next thirty years, never taking citizenship from any of the countries that offered it, he used both his trumpet and his voice to weave vivid, vibrant stories of a South Africa his heart was relentlessly determined to return to. In 1990, as the foundation of apartheid finally began to crack, the South African government relented and allowed him, and other freedom fighters like him, to finally come home. To be able to have shared Michael February's history-making moment with my father in his final days, on South African soil, is something I will treasure for the rest of my life.

With his success on the world stage as both a competitor and traveling free surfer now well-documented, Michael February is unlocking the portals of possibility for what the future of global surf culture will look like. Today's generation of young Black and African surfers do not have to look farther than their phones for inspiration to actively participate in a surfing lifestyle that has traditionally not included those who look like them. His must-watch two-part film *Sonic Souvenirs*, available on YouTube, is essentially a love note to Africa, affectionately exploring traditional African music, art, dance, and culture through the lens of Mikey's beautifully free-flowing approach to wave riding.

As stated earlier, I couldn't imagine what my surfing life as a young person would have been like with a Michael February existing in the world, so I asked a certified young person—my friend Brick, twenty-six—to contextualize it from his perspective.

"Mikey February is the lighthouse for our generation of surfers, especially those of African descent," Brick told me. "It's just nice to have someone to point to when explaining to my friends that don't surf, that this is what surfing looks like when it is performed at the highest level. When we see that person that looks like us, it makes it all feel that much more possible and achievable. To be able to witness Mikey is a blessing that inspires and informs my surfing and the people I surf with."

In his first heat at the 2023 Vans Pipe Masters, with the sun shining on an impossibly beautiful North Shore day, Michael February and three other competitors paddled out at the six-to-ten-foot Pipeline. Due to multiple swell directions in the water, conditions were oscillating somewhere between nearly perfect and wholly treacherous. The most seasoned big-wave surfers will tell you that they are in a constant dialogue with fear while surfing Pipeline. Michael is not the most seasoned big-wave surfer. He does not see the appeal in surfing places like Jaws or Waimea Bay, but something within him wholly believes he possesses both the skill set and the ability to meet the moment at Pipeline. So when given the opportunity to do so, he investigates that belief with a self-confidence tempered with patience and respect for the wave itself.

And so, as the thirty-five-minute heat clock ticks away, Mikey waits, avoiding getting drawn into the type of waves his fellow competitors are catching; instead patiently waiting for a wave that speaks directly to him. That wave ends up being a solid six-footer at Backdoor, the half of Pipeline that breaks to the right. The best Backdoor waves look unmakeable, as if they're going to eat you if you paddle for them. This is where the respect part kicks in, and Mikey, wasting no time, puts his head down and taps into the advantage of his very long arms to paddle with intention, get to his feet quickly, and deftly but also casually weave through the freight train of a heaving, multi-section barrel ride. The crowd cheers in approval, but Mikey has no time celebrate. The wave has spit him out into the dreaded space between Backdoor and its neighboring wave, Off the Wall, just as a massive set of ten-foot waves is about to unload squarely on Mikey February's head. Like the cool customer he is, Mikey somehow endures the five minutes or so of pure, unmitigated violence as wave after wave pummels him into the shallow reef below. Doing all he can to remain calm and preserve what little oxygen he has left, he survives the gargantuan pounding, with his body, board, and leash somehow intact.

And then, as if by decree of the universe, the ancestors, or a combination of both, while he makes the long paddle back out to the lineup, an even more perfect Backdoor wave swings wide of the pack and stands up right in front of him, leaving him no choice but to turn, paddle, and go. This wave is heavier than the first, with a heaving trifecta of multiple-barrel sections. Mikey pulls into the first section and responds to every attempt the wave makes to dismount him while he's inside the barrel. Five seconds later, he is gloriously spit out of the wave, arching in real-time slow motion, through the mist. It is unequivocally the wave of the day, garnering the loudest cheers up and down the beach, accompanied by the highest score of the event so far. A performance for the ages at the most iconic wave in the world.

About fifteen minutes later, after turning in his competition jersey to the beach marshal and fulfilling his post-heat media obligations, Michael February slowly makes his way back up the stone stairs, to the beachfront backyard doubling as the VIP and competitors' area. He is clearly exhausted, and for a moment seems almost unaware that he is at a contest. However, the deafening hoots, hollers, cheers, and sustained applause of those present snap him out of it. He stands there and takes a beat, head slightly down in deference to the moment, allowing himself a half smile. Out of the crowd walks his wife, Zelti, holding their young son. He kisses and hugs them both, and makes his way back to the staging area for his boards. There, I see him take a longer moment with himself, perhaps contemplating the beautiful uncertainty in all that has gotten him here and all that lies ahead.

*Tom Curren on May 19, 2023 at Morro Bay, San Luis Obispo, California. Photo by Anne Menke*

# 11.

## TOM CURREN

### By Chris Shiflett

*"They are like two sides of a coin. They're really different. Surfing, for me, it's the career path and less of a soulful thing, than somebody who surfs just for the pure experience. You have to get ready, train for events, practice, and things like that. And music is after hours and downtime. But the thing about surfing is that it's a rhythm of the waves coming in. It's a rhythm, and it's a reset. And you can wash off whatever stresses of life you have on land."*

CHRIS SHIFLETT, LEAD GUITARIST FOR THE FOO FIGHTERS, grew up in Santa Barbara, California, a coastal town recognized for its unique surf culture and geography. Santa Barbara is also known in the surf world for its hometown hero, three-time world champion Tom Curren, whose preternatural and inimitable style put him in the surf limelight in the 1980s, when he was just a teen, and helped put California at the forefront of contemporary surfing. Curren is still considered one of the all-time greatest by the greatest surfers in the world.

As a surfer himself, Shiflett knew of Curren, but the two never met growing up. By the time he got to high school, Curren was already a world champion, with the rock star status that Shiflett would later achieve in music. But in the early 1990s, Curren would leave the tour in his competitive prime to join the Rip Curl Search program, a marketing venture created to return surfing back to its free-spirited roots. This would become the foundation for director Sonny Miller's iconic film *Searching for Tom Curren*.

Curren was Shiflett's first choice to write about for *Surfer Stories*, not just because of his surfing but because of his cult of personality as well. There is also the fact that Curren is a musician himself. Needless to say, tracking Curren down for an interview was a challenge. But we made it happen…and they even went surfing together too, with photographer Anne Menke there to capture the session.

# FINDING TOM CURREN

## (INTERVIEW WITH TOM CURREN 5/19/23)

*"I walked home all the way from East Beach /
With an oil spill sticking to my feet."*

—from "West Coast Town," by Chris Shiflett

I can't exactly pinpoint the moment I first heard of Tom Curren. Even before I started surfing, his presence loomed large—three-time world champ, style master, and local Santa Barbara legend. As fate would have it, we grew up in the same part of town—the East side—but outside of a brief introduction at a Channel Islands Surfboards party years ago, I'd never met him. Although surf tends to be seasonal in Santa Barbara—lighting up in the winters, flat in the summers—surf *history* runs deep in our hometown. Reynolds "Renny" Yater, Al Merrick, Davey Smith, Bobby Martinez, the Coffin Brothers, Lakey Peterson, Shaun Tomson, and Kelly Slater are just a few of the famous names to have put their time in at local breaks like Hammond's and Rincon.

    Santa Barbara has also always suffered from tall poppy syndrome, and Tom Curren is without a doubt the tallest poppy to ever grow out of the

local surf scene. The word "enigma" is often used to describe him, even by friends and peers, so he remains a bit of a mystery, popping up occasionally in Heritage Heats at J-Bay or Bells, or in edits like Free Scrubber—experimenting with the strangest fins and boards but still carving perfect lines with his impeccable style.

Needless to say, I was a little nervous as I made my way up to his house, a couple hours north of Santa Barbara. Would I be able to pull some stories about the glory days out of him? Would he be willing to discuss the past? Did we have any overlap in our Santa Barbara experiences? I'd wondered if Tom's childhood bore any relation to my own—summers spent rooting around East Beach and Milpas Street, stealing candy out of the hotel lobbies along Cabrillo Boulevard, family beach days out on the sand in front of the Bathhouse, eating Mexican sweet bread from Salinas Market, late afternoons scraping tar off our feet, etc. Pulling into the driveway, I was greeted by his wife, Maki, who welcomed me in, and after brief introductions to Tom and their parrot, we sat down at their dining room table and settled in for a nice long chat.

**Chris Shiflett:** I was watching the remastered version of *Searching for Tom Curren* last night, and there's that great footage of you when you're really young, and a train's going by. Was that on the way down to Hammond's?

**Tom Curren:** Yeah.

**CS:** I knew it.

**TC:** Yep.

**CS:** Where's the surf footage from? It didn't look like Hammond's.

**TC:** That was Rincon. Well, it was mixed together. It was a few years after that.

*CS:* Who was filming you at that point? The really young stuff? Family? On Super 8 or something?

*TC:* No. This was a guy who was in Brooks Institute, and he had a school project.

*CS:* I had the exact same experience—when I was in my first bands in high school, we would always get Brooks students to take our promo pictures. I'm a couple years younger than you, but not much.

You grew up just off of Milpas, right? Next to Wilderness? Bob Duncan's place?

*TC:* That's right.

*CS:* I grew up on the East side, so same general vicinity. We bounced around a bit while my parents were still together, then once they were divorced, we wound up with my mom on Salinas Street around '77. My memory of that period of Santa Barbara was like, everybody's parents were shaggy-haired and smoking weed, and it just seemed like it was Fiesta or Summer Solstice all the time. What was it like for you? What do you remember about that time?

*TC:* That's right. The fiesta was great. And the rodeo was awesome. Santa Barbara, of course it wasn't as…what's the word? It wasn't the posh type of vibe and all that like up in Montecito, but was just a normal beach town, I guess.

*CS:* Yeah. Back then the East side was lower-middle-class, working-class, gritty…mostly Latino and white families. Santa Barbara wasn't the weekend destination for wealthy Los Angelenos that it is now. I love Santa Barbara—don't get me wrong—but it's changed in that respect.

*TC:* Yeah. It is just a little bit more out of reach for regular people, I guess. But there's always been Montecito and the big, beautiful houses.

We would always go up to the Bowl, which was a big skateboard mecca.

*CS:* Oh, the T-Bowls?

*TC:* Yeah. It was this giant reservoir. I don't know if you got any of that.

*CS:* I got that around junior high. That would've been the early '80s.

*TC:* Was that after they bombed it?

*CS:* It had already been bombed, but somebody had cleaned out the middle. And plus there were the Moguls, which were a little higher up.

*TC:* The Moguls. Yes!

*CS:* I wonder if that's still there now? It's probably been gotten rid of. There were two giant dirt piles and a clearing through the middle. I remember there was a pipe that you would try to skate up and over and do a big figure eight if you could.

*TC:* That's right.

*CS:* Did you get it when it was proper T-Bowls?

*TC:* Yeah. Prime time. Just the golden era. When [Tom] Sims was up there all the time—the Sims team. I would get free boards from Sims. He had his shop next to the high school.

*CS:* Oh, really? So, were you a sponsored skater even before you were a pro surfer?

*TC:* Not quite sponsored.

*CS:* That business model didn't exist quite yet?

TC: Well, it was a thing. There was the Sims team, and I really wanted to be on the Sims team. There was Davey Miller, Steve Monahan, Edie Robertson. I would get the blem boards, which were the boards that didn't come out quite right. They still worked fine, they're just the blems.

CS: Did Tom Sims ever pull you aside? Like, "Tom, if you keep messing around with this surfing thing, you're never going to be a pro skater." (*Laughs*)

TC: I don't know. I had one experience. We were up in Montecito with Sims and Stacy Peralta and this guy named Kenny Means, who was a roller skater. They were doing time trials down Hot Springs Road, and I was in the car. We used to go from the top of Cold Springs down to Hot Springs.

CS: Bombing it?

TC: Yeah. One time one of our friends went from Mountain Drive all the way to Hot Springs. And so, that opened the door. It was a great thing in summertime when the waves were not around. We would always skate in the summer and hitchhike around. A lot of skateboarding around Montecito. And surfing Hammond's a lot.

CS: How did your family wind up in Santa Barbara?

TC: We moved when I was six months old from Newport. My dad was in commercial diving, and my mom had a little bikini shop on Coast Village. That was in the early '70s.

CS: Did your dad come up to Santa Barbara because he was already friends with guys like [Renny] Yater and Bob Duncan? Were they all friends from the North Shore or something?

*Tom Curren in 1981 at Rincon Cove, Santa Barbara, California. Photo by Jimmy Metyko.*

# SURFER STORIES

*TC:* I don't actually know about all that, but he was working with a guy named Danny Mack, who's from Costa Mesa. And so, they came up for the diving.

*CS:* Out at the Channel Islands?

*TC:* Yeah. Abalone and then urchin diving, eventually.

*CS:* Your teenage years would have been wild, idyllic times in Santa Barbara. Before helicopter parenting. Just far enough away from LA that it felt like a small town but wasn't. I'm curious where you slotted in socially back then. Were you hanging out with the guys in RKL? At the bottle shop looking for keg parties on Friday night? Cruising IV?

*TC:* Not quite. As a youngster around sixth and seventh grade, we did that sort of thing. And then I went to the other extreme. I went to Christian school and got real serious about surfing at the same time.

*CS:* About how old were you?

*TC:* That was when I was around thirteen. At that point I was surfing the Pit quite a lot.

*CS:* And when did surfing start for you?

*TC:* Around 1970, when I was about six years old.

*CS:* Oh, young!

*TC:* Yeah.

*CS:* I read somewhere that you learned to surf at East Beach, which made me chuckle, if that's true, because East Beach was my local when I was a kid. I don't remember it being surfable at all. Is that really where you learned how to surf? (*Laughs*)

*TC:* No. That's impossible, really.

*CS:* That's what I thought.

*TC:* I think I've maybe surfed there once or twice, actually. But we were in the Junior Guards at East Beach. And that was a great time too, the Junior Guards.

*CS:* I would have been in Aqua Camp at that time.

*TC:* Yeah. Whenever I smell those…you remember corn strips?

*CS:* Sure.

*TC:* And the little sauce. That flavor brings back memories.

*CS:* Oh, yeah. The Bathhouse down at East Beach, and the smell of tar.

*TC:* Yes.

*CS:* My memory is walking home from East Beach and immediately getting out the Crisco oil to get the tar off my feet.

*TC:* That and, yeah, just certain songs that, you know, remind you of that time.

*CS:* Where did you start surfing?

*TC:* I started on a vacation trip to Hawaii, with a family trip over there, and then mainly Hammond's. And that was it, Hammond's and Miramar.

*CS:* How were you getting there when you were six years old?

*TC:* We lived in Montecito, off of Depot Road. If you're coming off the exit there, coming south, the very first little turnout off the off ramp, there were little cottages there.

*CS:* That was before the place off of Milpas?

*TC:* Correct.

*CS:* When I was in high school—you were probably gone already, off being a pro surfer—I was in a band with Alpo Duncan called Rat Pack, and we used to rehearse in his dad's shaping bay.

*TC:* That was our next-door neighbors.

*CS:* Yeah.

*TC:* That's incredible. Small world!

*CS:* I know. I remember being in there and just smelling the chemicals and not really understanding what it was. "What is all this shit? Is your dad a lifeguard or something?" (*Laughs*)

*TC:* As funny as it sounds, I used to get complaints from Bob, his dad, for playing the drums.

*CS:* Oh, really?

*TC:* Too loud, and too early in the morning. That little neighborhood was right in between the train tracks and the freeway. It was like the last little bit. Now, it's just a roundabout, one of those big roundabout freeway exits, and the whole thing is not there anymore.

*CS:* I noticed that a while ago. It's sad.

Was music always something that was happening in parallel with your surfing? I mean, for people that don't know, you're a really good musician, a great guitar player, great singer. I know you play keys and stuff too, and maybe a little bit of everything. But your guitar playing's solid.

*TC:* I appreciate that.

*CS:* It doesn't sound like you picked that up later in life. Was that something you were doing at the same time as surfing?

*TC:* Yeah. I started playing guitar in a youth group. Had a youth pastor there who was a great guitarist and knew every Beatles song, everything from Simon & Garfunkel. He was a great mentor, Steve Yamaguchi. That was when I was around thirteen or fourteen. And I've been playing the drums since I was about seven, maybe younger, if you include silverware and [the] couch.

*CS:* Banging on Tupperware and whatnot?

*TC:* I was always playing the drums. But I guess, for me, when I wanted to progress as a guitar player was when I heard Steve Cropper.

*CS:* Mmm, sure. Was your introduction The Blues Brothers?

*TC:* Kind of. But Steve Cropper just made me think, "Wow! I want to do that. I think I can do that." Nowadays, when you hear some of his playing, it's so right—the rhythm playing.

*CS:* Who else were you listening to? Your first record, it's more instrumental, almost like Steely Dan–flavor, jazzy stuff. And then that last record you put out is way more song-driven. I hear shades of everything from Jackson Browne to Pink Floyd in there, especially with your guitar playing. Sounds like I hear some Gilmour in there.

*TC:* Oh, thanks. I had help on those. I had some other people playing there. Maybe the Pink Floyd that you're hearing was not me.

*CS:* Ah!

*TC:* But yes—definitely Steely Dan. I was very into Steely Dan. And then just classic British blues rock. Grand Funk. Deep Purple.

**CS:** I get asked all the time, "What's the connection between surfing and music?" And for me, there is zero connection. The two things couldn't be further apart. Music is my job, and it's a great job, but it's wrapped up in ego and ambition and commerce and all the ugly shit that goes along with all that stuff. Whereas surfing has none of that for me. I'm never going to get paid to ride a surfboard. It's also the one place in modern life where I'm truly disconnected and in the moment. To me, it's the great escape. And I'm a mediocre surfer anyway, just trying to get down the face of the wave, get a couple pumps in…ya know what I mean? Do you have a similar thing in reverse? Is there a parallel for you, creatively?

**TC:** Yes. I tend to agree with that. They are like two sides of a coin. They're really different. Surfing, for me, it's the career path and less of a soulful thing, than somebody who surfs just for the pure experience. You have to get ready, train for events, practice, and things like that. And music is after hours and downtime. But the thing about surfing is that it's a rhythm of the waves coming in. It's a rhythm and it's a reset. And you can wash off whatever stresses of life you have on land.

**CS:** Have you ever tried teaching one of your friends that's from Nebraska or London or somewhere how to surf? I've tried that a couple of times, and if you don't have that intuitive sense of the rhythm of the ocean, that's the hardest part to lock in with.

**TC:** Right. The thing about surfing is, you can't really fight against the waves.

**CS:** Yeah. Because you lose, every time.

Is surfing a creative outlet for you, similar to music?

*TC:* Well, if I was out practicing, and you have a song in your head—the best parts of the song, really juicy guitar playing or something—you focus in on something like that. It's always been a creative outlet, surfing. And I think a lot of that more nowadays is developed into board design.

*CS:* You're well-known for being experimental in the extreme with fins and skim boards and slicing things off of conventional shapes.

*TC:* Yeah. I've never been a surfboard shaper, but I've always been what my friend calls "a tinkerer."

*CS:* Did you have a lot of back-and-forth as a kid with Al Merrick? I know you worked closely with Channel Islands for a long time and are still part of that family. Can you talk a little bit about the impact he had, not just on you as a person, but also your surfing craft and technique?

*TC:* Certainly. Al was hugely important for how well I was able to do. And he has this mastery of board design.

*CS:* I never hear anybody talk about his actual surfing. And I don't think I've ever *seen* a picture of him surfing. Would he be out there coaching you?

*TC:* Yes. He was surfing a lot. He was a great surfer too. When he was younger, before we met, he was at pro level actually, before he got into the shaping thing. His designs benefited *because* he was a great surfer, and so he would be making boards for us and then dialing it in on his own at Rincon.

*CS:* When did Rincon enter the picture for you?

*TC:* Well, I was from Hammond's and then eventually got rides down to Rincon. I would say somewhere around '73.

*CS:* So, how old would you have been at that point?

*TC:* About eight or nine.

*CS:* And was Rincon home base for the whole Channel Islands team? Weren't they based out there?

*TC:* Yeah. Channel Islands was in town, but Al lived in Carpenteria.

*CS:* Did he see you surfing Rincon as a kid, and then ask you to start riding for him?

*TC:* Initially, the manager of the shop, Kim Robinson, recommended me to talk to Al. I knew him at Hammond's. And he said, "See if Tom wants to get a board or something," and then we worked it out. I worked at the shop there, then cleaning the shaping room, and then I got my first board. I think it was around '77. Before that, I was just riding whatever, just oddball boards. And then before that, it was my dad who made my boards.

*CS:* I read somewhere your dad didn't teach you how to surf, or wasn't involved. Is that true?[3]

*TC:* No. That's not quite true. My mom was more involved with getting me to the competitions and on that side of it, but the experience with my dad surfing was very impactful, because we would surf in San Diego. I remember we surfed out at Sunset Cliffs, and it was sizeable, and I was pretty little. And I remember my dad—I don't think he had a leash. And actually, we both lost our boards, and they washed out to sea.

---

3   Tom's father, Pat Curren, was a renowned board shaper and big-wave rider in the '50s and '60s. He was one of the early pioneers of the North Shore of Hawaii.

CS: Really?

TC: Yeah. We left without our boards.

CS: Oh, man! How big was it?

TC: It was around eight to ten feet, probably.

CS: And how old were you?

TC: I don't know. Ten or twelve years old.

CS: Wow! That's meaty for a ten-year-old.

TC: Yes. It was one of those really just glassy, approachable days. It was too big for me, but he was there. We lost our boards, we swam, and we got caught in the rip. I managed to get around that, and I just remember trying to do a bottom turn and I couldn't do it, because I couldn't tell where the bottom of the wave was. It was one of those reef breaks out there.

CS: Before the double-pump bottom turn had come into play?

TC: That's right.

CS: Santa Barbara back then was black wetsuit, white board, stoic, not the most welcoming lineups in the world. So, being your dad's son, were you welcomed at that young age into those lineups?

TC: I didn't really have any issues.

CS: But I think in those days it was like, "You can't surf here. Go into the kiddy break, or we're going to stuff you in the trash can." Did you have to go through that sort of hazing?

TC: I don't actually remember anything like that. We had a crew there at Hammond's, a regular crew. And they were good folks, and it was like its own little environment there. The meadow was twice as

big as it is now, and it was a little community back there. And it was where we'd hang out a lot, and they were taking care of me, actually.

**CS:** Who were some of the local surfers in Santa Barbara that would've been an influence on you, that were never pro, never famous, that the world has never heard of?

**TC:** Oh, well one person who comes to mind is Dale Deller. He was a great surfer. And there's Kippy Harmer. And that was just the Hammond's crew. And then I remember the guys from the Pit would come to Hammond's sometimes, and they would go left. They were ripping, just more progressive.

**CS:** Do you get out to Hammond's much nowadays?

**TC:** No.

**CS:** I imagine it was a lot less crowded back then?

**TC:** Right. Yeah. But on a good winter swell, if it's consistent, then it seems to be less crowded sometimes.

**CS:** Yeah. You can still get one of those magic mornings if you trudge down there early enough. I was out at Rincon a couple winters ago. It would've been right after Free Scrubber came out. It was a good day, and it was really crowded, and you paddled through the lineup. I was up around Indicator and you paddled through. And I remember the guy that was closest to me, we both look at each other and go, "That's Tom Curren!"

All these years later, anytime you're out, all eyes are on you. Can you reflect on that a little bit? What does that feel like?

**TC:** Well, it's a nice thing to be recognized for doing something well. It doesn't really get me more waves, though.

*CS:* Really?

*TC:* I don't really like to drop in on people.

*CS:* Are people dropping in on you?

*TC:* No.

*CS:* Well, that's worth something right there.

*TC:* I learned a funny little trick about that. When you're coming through the top of the cove and you see somebody paddling way down there, with their head down, and they're just going to go? If you pretend you're going to stall for a barrel, they will pull back.

*CS:* Really?

*TC:* Yeah. That's the trick.

*CS:* I thought they just didn't look over their left shoulder. (*Laughs*)

*TC:* That's right. But I've tried it a couple times and it worked, because they would think, "Uh-oh, this thing is ledging out." And it's like, "Uh-oh."

*CS:* That is a serious pro tip right there.

Backing up a little bit…. When did the competition side of surfing enter for you? And why do you think you took to that so well?

*TC:* I started competing when I was around thirteen and a half, fourteen. Actually, I'd been in the little WSA events before that, and I didn't do well. But once I got a win and I won pretty solidly, that was a good one to say, "Well, I like this." And I guess the experience at Junior Guards was helpful there. And then swim team, being on swim team at high school. So, those are a couple things that were important for me as far as competitiveness.

*CS:* You're famously credited as the person that brought a new athleticism to pro surfing, where before it was people partying all the time, which I'm sure was still going on, but you weren't really a part of that, right?

*TC:* Yes. I was serious about that. Very focused, and I guess it's a way to stay away from distractions as well. And even if there were no waves, just go and stand in waist-deep water with your board and splash around and wait for something to come in.

*CS:* When did you become a full-time, traveling, professional surfer?

*TC:* Well, my pro career started in 1982.

*CS:* Were you still in high school at that point?

*TC:* Just finished high school.

*CS:* Was all that attention—and having some understanding of your personality—what ultimately led you to move to Europe? Was it just too much of a lens on you all the time?

*TC:* I don't know. I think, like you said, Santa Barbara is definitely a surf town, but it's a seasonal thing. So, surfing in the winter and skateboarding in the summer wouldn't really work.

*CS:* Was there much of a surf scene in France when you got there?

*TC:* Definitely a surf scene. And we went for the amateur titles in 1980. And it was in September, and we got off the plane, got on the bus, and pulled up, and there was just amazing surf. It was like, "Wow!"

*CS:* "I never want to leave."

*TC:* And that was 1980. Later I had family ties over there, and so I was spending more time over there, and that was the home base. I would do training and just go to the weight room and everything. The other thing was, I always admired the Australians, and the vibe with the Australians was a very competitive atmosphere. They're very surf-oriented, and so I wanted to emulate that a bit. The Australians had a real professional approach.

*CS:* They behaved like pro athletes?

*TC:* Yeah. So, I wanted to do well. I was always trying to emulate that.

*CS:* Were you friendly with guys like Mark Richards back then?

*TC:* Yeah. So back in 1982 I went to Australia for the first time, and I think the year after that, I met Mark Richards. I was just a quiet kid, and these people were larger than life for me.

*CS:* But a quiet kid that, I'm assuming at that time, had the reputation that you were the guy that was coming to take their crown. How did the older guard handle you coming into their scene?

*TC:* Yeah. I guess you have to push a little bit and you have to be aggressive. There was definitely a lot of kids my age in Australia who were—it was almost more of a natural thing for Australians. The whole lifestyle or culture actually is rooted in competition in a lot of ways. And then the older Australians that I knew, like Wayne Lynch and Nat Young, they did a 180 and said, "Well, I don't compete. I don't like it; I think it's wrong." But in 1982, when we went to the world amateurs in Queensland, there was actually newspaper coverage of the contest. So that was something that we were not used to.

*CS:* Mainstream media covering surfing?

*TC:* Yep—the sports page reporting on the event.

*Tom Curren and Chris Shiflett on May 19, 2023 at Morro Bay, San Luis Obispo, California.*
*Photos by Anne Menke*

*CS:* Did you have a sense of pro surfing growing in real time, all around you? Any sense of where it would eventually get in the '90s? Did you sense that you were part of that evolution taking place?

*TC:* That's a good question. It's hard to say. I'm not quite sure I was thinking the sport of surfing would grow exponentially, as it did. I would say I thought it was—again, Australia was taking it more like a regular sport, and it's always been like that in Australia, and in California we were playing catch-up a little bit. But I thought the events were big back then, and they were.

*CS:* Did you spend a lot of time on the North Shore in those years too? Did you ever live over there full-time?

*TC:* No. I would just go over there in the winter. Most of the news that we got was from surf movies. And one movie in particular, *Free Ride*, was inspiring in the way that it featured Rabbit [Bartholomew] and his day-to-day thing.

*CS:* It's so different now with social media. In those days, how would you learn the new maneuvers? Would you have to wait until a movie came out? Would it get passed along from local scene to local scene?

*TC:* Yeah, that's right. We pretty much had to wait for a movie to come our way. And then, of course, it would mean that it was at least six months, or maybe a year later, that we would get the intel. But I think the attitude for contest surfing changed quickly. This one movie *Five Summer Stories* had a different opinion about contest surfing. It's very anti-contest. They showed a contest in Huntington and just painted a picture of this really gross commercialism.

*CS:* That's been there for a long time in surfing, and still is to some extent. It reminds me of the punk rock world of the '90's, when I was young and coming up, where there was this real heavy debate about major labels versus indies. If you did the major-label thing, you were a sellout. There's some kind of parallel there.

*TC:* Yeah, that's true. I think the old school were wary of surfing in contests and they didn't—in California anyways. Australia was different, and then Hawaii was different too. Hawaii is where surfing came from. But the competitive side of surfing is very linked with Hawaiian surfing, because it was part of the whole thing in Hawaii. And so, now that I think about it, it's just a part of surfing. And even if you don't like competing, if you're going to try to go surf Rincon, you're competing anyways.

*CS:* Right. You're competing with your friends if nothing else. (*Laughs*)

*TC:* You have to. So when I hear people say, "I hate contests," if you want to get any waves, you have to be competitive in some way, right?

*CS:* But ultimately, you grew tired of competing too. What was the end of the line that made you want to leave the tour?

*TC:* The part for me that was hard was the progression of surfing into aerials and things like that, where I was picturing that things would change so fast that I wouldn't be able to keep up. That was part of it. And then, just outside interests.

*CS:* That's really interesting, because I feel like, and maybe I'm wrong here, but that period after you won your last title in '90, and that next stretch through the '90s, was your most influential period. Am I right in thinking that?

*TC:* I suppose, yeah. It had to do with the filming that we did with Sonny Miller.

CS: The Search?

TC: The Search. It just unblocked a lot of things in a way.

CS: Things you couldn't do in contest surfing?

TC: Yeah. Riding different kinds of boards and just looking for swells and things like that. And for me, I really had to be 150 percent all the time to feel like I had the confidence to compete. So, it was liberating in a lot of ways, for sure.

CS: What do you think of as your greatest strength when you were in your prime?

TC: I guess the thing for me was that I was able to go out in ordinary waves and find a good one.

CS: When you were first coming up, could you have ever imagined still having a pro career all these years later?

TC: I really don't think so.

CS: Where did you think it would wind up back in those days?

TC: You think of how your value to your sponsors is based on your competitive results. And so, you start thinking about how you're going to keep going and maybe getting a surf shop going or anything like that, just to figure out something in surfing. And it was always a little bit of an anxious subject, because you want to keep surfing, and you know that you have to fit in somewhere in the industry. Ideally, you could go around and make movies, or do something to just be able to sustain that lifestyle. And it worked out for me. I had the support from Rip Curl for so many years, and they had a good, organic approach. They did The Search, and it was actually connected to the company. The company was pretty core, I guess.

# TOM CURREN | 235

**CS:** If you were a sixteen-year-old kid coming up today, where everybody's got to be their own brand, creating constant content, would you have slotted right in? Or would you have suffered in today's environment?

**TC:** It has changed so much. I don't know. I did well because of the support I had. I mean, I had to do my part, but the support, it made it possible. So now, when I think of how you have to carve your own path and create an identity and things like that, it's very foreign to me. I guess I don't know how I would do.

**CS:** One last thing. In watching *Searching for Tom Curren* last night, there's that part towards the end where it says, "This is not intended to be the definitive history." It begs the question, where's the Tom Curren definitive history?

**TC:** Mm-hmm. Oh, I don't know.

**CS:** I think the world needs that.

**TC:** Maybe.

**CS:** Wisdom from on high. Or just loads and loads of great footage through the years. Either way, I think the world needs the definitive history.

**TC:** I thought maybe one day I would write a book or something.

**CS:** I think we just did.

**TC:** That's right.

**CS:** That was a lot of fun.

**TC:** Thank you.

**CS:** Let's go get some waves.

*Kelly Slater in 1990 on the North Shore of Oahu, Hawaii. Photo by Tom Servais*

# 12.

## KELLY SLATER

## By Shaun Tomson

*"In 1989, when I first saw him surf, Kelly was a compact and slender nut-brown Cocoa Beach, Florida kid, brown hair flecked with blond streaks, with a fluro orange Matt Kechele board, a color-coordinated fluro green O'Neill wetsuit, and an aura of absolute confidence. His style was fluid and fast and unlike any young surfer I had ever seen, quick yet calm, powerful yet loose, fully realized and fully ready—already able to channel the elusive state of flow. It was like he had it all, already: an aura of imperturbability, a calmness and mental quietness, and right then I could see he was going to take surfing down an entirely new road—and scarily, I think he knew it too."*

Surfing great Shaun Tomson is one of the first generation of pro surfers, an icon of the '70s and '80s, who won nineteen major pro contests and the world championship in 1977. Tomson writes about this generation's surf icon Kelly Slater, who is widely considered the GOAT—Greatest of All Time. Slater has been on the pro tour since 1991, winning the world title in his rookie year in 1992, and has dominated pro surfing ever since, with such stats as: eleven world titles, five of them consecutive, and being the oldest at thirty-nine and youngest at twenty to win a world title, among many more record-breaking achievements.

"No sportsman in the world anywhere has for so many years been so far ahead of his peers—not Tiger, Ali, Jordan, LeBron, Gretzky, or Federer/Nadal/Djokovic," says Tomson, as he also writes of Slater's pure "stoke" for surfing that has made him one of the fiercest and most dominating competitors in any sport.

# IN THE MOMENT

*"Don't ever count yourself out."*
*It was this mantra that I came up with.*
*I can only be.*
*I can only control myself in the moment.*
*I don't know what's going to happen.*
*Enjoy this thing—you're in the place you've wanted to be*
*your whole life.*
*This is where I wanted to be when I was eight or ten years old,*
*and I'm here, and I'm in this, and even if I lose.*
*You know what, you're fucking lucky to be here.*
*So, I remember just focusing and thinking, Kelly, put your hand*
*in the water and feel that paddle and feel that, and be here.*
*Just be here right now.*
*And I paddled back out. And I think I got like a 9.5*
*on the next wave.*
*Instead of getting too excited about that, I went,*
*You know the thing that got you there was being present*
*being in the moment.*
*So just stay here.*
*I ended up winning the contest.*
*I took that, and I ran with it.*
*It helped me be present with people, with my competition*
*with the world, with my life."*
—Kelly Slater, October 2023

Some years ago, I drove down from Santa Barbara to the leafy California town of Claremont, through the wide streets bordered by Craftsman-style homes, and presented a talk on purpose and performance to the Western Positive Psychology Association at Claremont Graduate University. I had lunch with Professor Emeritus Mihaly Csikszentmihalyi, a renowned Hungarian American psychologist who created the term "flow" to describe a mental state in which a person performing an activity is fully immersed in a feeling of energized focus, involvement, and enjoyment in the moment and in the process. According to Csikszentmihalyi, flow is characterized by complete absorption in what one does, often resulting in the loss of a sense of time and self-consciousness.

The best athletes experience this rarified state of complete focus on their performance, with no attention to distractions or irrelevant thoughts. The mind is wholly occupied by the activity, contributing to enhanced performance. Athletes in flow feel a sense of elation and fulfillment. They experience heightened enjoyment and satisfaction in their performance, further fueling their commitment and concentration. Activities seem spontaneous and effortless. Athletes feel as though they are "in the zone," and their movements and decisions come naturally without forced effort. In a flow state, athletes lose awareness of themselves as separate from the activity they are performing, feeling as though time has either sped up or slowed down.

Over the last fifty years, I have watched many of the greatest athletes with an appreciation for their commitment, instincts, fire, technique, and talent. Only the very best seem to be able to click into flow at will, that elevated state of consciousness necessary to perform beyond their perceived best. In my assessment, Kelly Slater is a master of flow, a unique and extraordinary athlete deeply and intimately connected to the rhythm and flow of the ocean, his consciousness, and the people in his orbit.

# KELLY SLATER

In all the world's sports, surfing stands alone for its unpredictability and vastness, unbounded by white lines of demarcation—a surfer standing atop an ever-changing medium, balanced upon an invisible pulse of energy. Maneuvers and techniques have evolved over the past thirty years, but the essential DNA of truly great surfing is unchanged; a few simple words define its essence: speed, power, rhythm, aggression, style, and imagination. Kelly has all this, and he has that extra chromosome of intuition, a knowingness, a prescient reactivity to the ebb and flow of the ocean. In competition, his wave selection is uncanny, inextricably linked to a connectivity and understanding of the ocean's energy while he is in the moment, in his flow state.

I was part of the first generation of pro surfers, winning nineteen major pro contests, including the World Pro title in 1977, and enjoying a long career that stretched through the '70s and into the '80s, ending with my retirement in December 1989. As a hard-core and analytical competitor, it was my job to evaluate anyone new coming up through the ranks, as I liked to be forewarned of upcoming opposition. I distinctly remember the first time I saw the '70s surf greats—Mark Richards and Rabbit Bartholomew and the '80s young Turks—Mark Occhilupo, Martin Potter, Tom Curren, and Tom Carroll. All of them made a strong first impression, and all had a special spark, potential waiting to be realized, a future that was going to be written in bold capital letters.

I always believed that I saw Kelly Slater for the first time in December 1989 at the red-hot center of surfing, on the North Shore of Oahu, as I was departing the world pro tour. He was just seventeen, and I was double his age—two surfing generations between us. In a recent Zoom call, Kelly, with a memory that misses nothing, corrects my timeline: "I first met you in the early eighties—I was a stoked grommet, and I got your autograph."

In 1989, when I first saw him surf, Kelly was a compact and slender nut-brown Cocoa Beach, Florida kid, brown hair flecked with blond streaks, with a fluro orange Matt Kechele board, a color-coordinated fluro green O'Neill wetsuit, and an aura of absolute confidence. His style was fluid and fast and unlike any young surfer I had ever seen, quick yet calm, powerful yet loose, fully realized and fully ready—already able to channel the elusive state of flow. It was like he had it all, already: an aura of imperturbability, a calmness and mental quietness, and right then I could see he was going to take surfing down an entirely new road—and scarily, I think he knew it too.

Kelly Slater's competitive statistics numb the brain, absolutely overwhelm it with the breadth and depth of his achievements. He qualified for the tour in 1991, won the title in his rookie year in 1992, and since then has systematically destroyed every competitive record out there, erasing from the record books every other name from every generation of the sport, including Mark Richards (four consecutive world titles), Tom Curren (most event wins, with thirty-three), and Mark Occhilupo (oldest world champ, at thirty-three). He has built a grand edifice of success that will cast a long shadow over everyone that comes in his wake: eleven world titles, five of them consecutive; being the oldest, at thirty-nine, and the youngest, at twenty, to win a world title, and the oldest to win a world tour event at forty-nine; fifty-six ASP event wins, eight Pipeline Masters wins, and $2.2 million in prize money.

No sportsman in the world anywhere has for so many years been so far ahead of his peers—not Tiger, Ali, Jordan, LeBron, Gretzky, or Federer/Nadal/Djokovic. None of these greatest sportsmen of all time has come close to his record of total dominance, yet in the grand expanse of mainstream sport, his genius is relatively obscure, because surfing is still a relatively obscure sport. While not attaining the popular recognition or enormous wealth of other pro athletes, he is still a marketer's dream—articulate, intelligent, handsome. Outside of the surfing industry, there are few mainstream sponsorships—no car, credit card, beverage, or food companies. He has an interest in a sustainable clothing line, Outerknown, an alliance with Breitling watches, and a financial interest in the World Surf League via the Kelly Slater Wave Company, a manmade wave park that is transforming the sport.

A number of years back, he was paid very well by his longtime sponsor Quiksilver, which made a fortune marketing his image from Shanghai to Stalingrad. Then a new CEO came in with a new marketing officer, who questioned spending all that money on a forty-year-old bald guy. Word on the street was that the CEO kept Kelly waiting for three hours to discuss a new deal. Kelly's deal evaporated, and within a few months, the publicly traded Quiksilver started to evaporate too, losing more than $250 million in stock value as the shares plunged. In short order, the CEO and his CMO were let go, and Quiksilver has yet to recover.

Kelly has a cheerful ruthlessness in him, an animal cunning that is very well concealed beneath the charisma and compact stature. And the competitive fire is always bubbling there, just below the surface. You get the feeling that Kelly never makes the same mistake twice. He has the same absolute confidence he displayed at seventeen and is able to turn a heat around at any moment. Kelly is currently a long way from another win—he is recuperating from surgery on a nagging hip injury. His last world title was in 2011, and his last major contest win was the Billabong Pipeline Pro in 2022, one of the greatest wins of his career—as a competitor ages, the wins are more sparing but intensely sweeter.

While time impacts every aging athlete's consistency, it hasn't dulled Kelly's competitive fire and desire to be at the center of the surfing world's attention. At the 2022 Billabong Pipeline Pro, the world's most prestigious and challenging event, Kelly rolled back the years, pulling off miraculous wins and a complex tube ride where he vanished for several seconds while racing across the razor-sharp coral reef, emerging to the roar of the crowd, while competing against surfers half his age. And he never ever gave up, in seemingly impossible situations; he stayed in the flow, stayed in the moment, and won.

At fifty-one now, Kelly is still in great shape, redefining what is possible in the sport, and he is still improving. He is a natural-born carver, and his powers are fully realized on long walls at Jeffreys Bay or Bells or in epic tubes, backside or frontside. On the wide expanse at Jeffreys, his surfing is very radical and progressive, based around swooping turns off the bottom and very tight and late arcs off the top—he still does the unexpected, and sometimes, instead of running out his turn around the falling lip, he hits it full-on, busting the tail free in a controlled power drive, reacting with lightning-quick reflexes. He maintains a low center of gravity, crouches low through the turn, and then gets the spring and projection as the concave releases from the downward pressure.

Kelly has always had a special connection with J-Bay in South Africa, the world's longest, fastest world tour venue—a connectivity unlike anyone I have ever seen. There is some sort of sublime, deeper relationship there, hidden beneath the surfing you see on the surface. He has a connectedness to the environment, an enlightenment, a rare understanding of how he fits into the natural order of life, and it shines through him brightly.

"The first day I was ever there," he tells me, "I saw dolphins, I saw a shark, whales, flamingos, all within just a few minutes of being there. So that really struck me. It just seemed like a place that was so alive. So much happening, so much going on with the wildlife, and then, when you go out, you're just a part of that. I mean, the closest I've ever been to whales has been there. There've been a lot of waves with dolphins too. In fact, in that epic final I had with Andy Irons in 2005, before I won, before my last wave, there were dolphins going back out. And I was so tired; I was so out of my mind, with just about two minutes left in the final. I'd almost given up, just because physically I didn't have much strength left, and I said, 'Well, I'll just follow these dolphins.' And I paddled right behind the dolphins all the way back out. And it was something pretty magical, and it was the last thought I had before I got that wave, that won it for me with thirty-two seconds left. That's when you wonder what that deeper connection is to nature and stuff, because I literally just said, 'I'll just follow these dolphins.' I was thinking in my head, 'They'll take me to the right place.' And they did."

Kelly has an interesting take on the nexus of competition and creativity. In surfing, there is a tug of war between competitive surfing and free surfing—surfing as an artistic and soulful endeavor unencumbered by rules, points, and judging compared with surfing as a means to achieve victory over an opponent. Some think of competition as mechanistic, without creativity, but Kelly sees his path differently.

"No one really thinks of competition as creativity. But I'll tell you. I feel like I was really creative competitively to be able to win as much as I was in different ways. I hate to think that, on one level, my competition record is like my best addition to the surf world. But it taught me a lot about myself, and it taught me a lot about problem solving. *What's this challenge I have with this person? What's this hole I've dug for myself here? How do I get myself out of it?* There are so many times I've been in this situation where I'm like, *If I just incrementally get back in this thing, I'll win.*"

But losses have gotten to him. In retrospect he has adopted a philosophical perspective, viewing defeat as a learning experience. There are a couple of losses that have even been more profound to him than the wins. Dealing with the disappointment of defeat has been part of his learning and development. Every wave, every loss, every win is all part of a process of improving himself not only as a surfer but as a person.

"You know, the intensity of competition doesn't seem like a spiritual place, but the lessons it's taught me have shown me a lot about myself over the years. If you lose a contest or world title, really at the end of the day, it's not that important. And that was a lesson I learned when I lost in 2003 to Andy at Pipe. In that moment, I was devastated, and it was just a crushing defeat because it was so close. But I just know that if I could go back right now and switch it, I would lose again, because it just made me a better person. It's hard, and even saying that's kind of emotional for me, because how do you let something go that you want and love so much and be OK with that? I'm not a religious person by any means, but it was a godsend, it was a gift, because of what came from it, even though a lot of it was heavy, bad, and a horrible feeling. It allowed me to come back stronger, and it made me feel a lot closer with people in my world and all the guys I have competed against for so long."

But beyond the contest stats and the creative competing is the purely inspirational surfing that is often overlooked, if that can be possible. He revolutionized backside tube riding, particularly at Pipeline.[4] He created an entirely new drop-knee, grab-rail style that enabled him to take off far later than anyone ever before, stab the rail of the boards into the face, and slow down mid-face, holding and changing his line through the tube, turning a disadvantage into a strength. The biggest change in surfing, the fundamental shift from the all-power movement of the '70s and '80s, was his power-and-release approach, which entirely opened up surfing above the wave. He was one of the first to regularly incorporate the aerial as a functional maneuver in his repertoire as a result of this seismic shift in his approach. He singlehandedly boosted surfing into this new age; there is surfing B.K. and surfing A.K.

Riding the tube is an art form. Kelly has this special gift of slowing down time and finding his way out of seemingly impossible situations. I built my

---

4   A surfer either faces the wave or rides with their back to the wave—frontside or backside. At Pipeline, the world's most dangerous wave, riding backside was always presumed to be a disadvantage. Riding frontside enables more delicate adjustments through pressure applied through one's toes—a lot more difficult on one's heels.

# KELLY SLATER | 247

surfing in the '70s around expanding time and rewriting the lines that could be drawn in the tube. Kelly created a whole new art form in the '90s with a relaxed fearlessness and casual bravado, accelerating through impossible sections, at home in the eye of the hurricane.

"So many things in nature resemble a tube, a tornado, or a hurricane, or a galaxy. It's a natural sort of shape. And they say that the eye of the hurricane is the safest place to be. And the tube is really the eye of the hurricane in the water. But then you have the foam ball or tube monster, as we call it, always trying to get you, and if you can flirt with that and play with that, that's really the ultimate barrel ride—to be able to ride on the foam ball and have your tail drift out and still have the wave pushing you along. It's really the ultimate feeling of surfing, that and just getting lifted off your board by spit and landing back on it, or having your board track out because of it, because all that energy is lifting the tail out. Probably the most incredible feeling I've ever had is where you actually get behind the foam ball, where the lip is landing that creates a little void in the water, and you can actually get your board on that, and it will just pull you right through the barrel. You don't have to do anything: you don't have to react; you don't have to move. Once you do, you get on this track and you are on cruise control, on autopilot, and you don't have to do a lot; the wave will pull you along at its own speed. It feels like there is a rope on the nose of my board pulling me along."

It seems there is a trend on the pro surfing tour to surf much more upright, with a more stiffened lower back, but Kelly is all rubber-like flexibility that in essence mirrors his approach to life. His style comes naturally. It is instinctive.

"Style is what naturally comes out of your body. I think to be concerned about style is kind of egocentric, to be honest with you, if it's anything forced—if you're trying to make it look a certain way, whether you're going out at night and the clothes you wear, or if you are riding a wave and the way you hold your hands and your arms. If you're doing anything besides what comes naturally, it's not real. It's not you. When you're surfing, you see the wave, you stand up, you get from here to there, and the way you get from here to there without thinking about it, that's your style, and that's what you should stick with."

Listening to Kelly speak, calm and unhurried, one gets the impression of thoughtfulness, humor, and a sense of history. He is complex, quite guarded, severely analytical internally, humble on the exterior yet with a desire to be at the center of attention, whether in a surf contest final or just sitting on a bench with a guitar entertaining a raucous crowd throughout the night. He is goal-oriented but performance-focused, and this seems to be one of his secrets. He doesn't have a rigid, structured plan of physical training and coaching building him toward winning the title. He has the curiosity and humility of a lifelong learner—always striving for more and to be better. Kelly lives right in that moment and that decision, and letting go of structure and the ending seems to give him peace, confidence, and energy. But even with all his experience and this positive mindset, he still feels the pressure.

"I think athletes who are able to win big tournaments all have this thing where they can do it better or bigger, faster, or whatever. A lot of that comes on the really small, minute details, but I don't really feel anything is expected of me so much as it was when I was younger. I don't think about it as much either, as if I have to surf to a certain level. But when I'm out surfing with the best guys, I feel like at that point definitely—my head is on the chopping block. It's like you've got to step up and perform, and you're either on those guys' level or you are way down below. And at those times, I think all of us get our confidence rocked a little bit with a bad heat or even a silly turn on a wave. So, there's always this constant yearning to better your performance and go somewhere you haven't gone."

On no wave does he feel that pressure more than at Pipeline. To him, Pipeline is the most important wave in the surfing universe. It's the spot where everyone is watching. Everyone is focused on it. Everyone sees everything that happens. They're all part of the action. That's the excitement of the place.

"Pipeline is like no other place in the world. It's the most intense scene in the world of surfing, because you have so many good guys and you have a hundred photographers. There's all kinds of pecking orders happening, not only with pro surfers: locals against guys that don't live here, against pros, against amateurs, against groms and girls and bodyboarders. And then you've got a pecking order between photographers, where they can sit deeper or get priority amongst themselves, and guys bodysurfing. It's a funny scene, because all this energy is focusing in one little place at one time, and it's just an intense thing. And then, you've got to put yourself in some of the most dangerous waves that we surf on a big day, and everything is right there in your face. Obviously, at places like Sunset, Haleiwa, Waimea, those are all testing—those are proving grounds, but they're all further from the beach. Waimea only breaks once in the blue moon. You're caught inside by a fifteen-foot wave at Sunset, and no one on the beach knew. You get caught inside on a fifteen-foot wave at Pipe, and everyone sees it. If you don't have confidence at a place like Pipeline, it's going affect you, especially if you're going for the world title. You have got to know that increases your pressure."

It used to be a little lonely for the greatest surfer of all time, out there in his self-created stratosphere. He traveled the world constantly, surfed in ten contests a year at some of the world's greatest surfing locations, was surrounded by thousands of adoring fans, but those in his inside circle, his crew that he used to travel and surf and compete with, were pretty much all gone from his daily life. Even his many rivals had hung it up or been pushed out by the relentless advancement of youth and newness. It's just plain hard to get old on the pro tour, and new surfers just come at you from every country, from every direction, like legions advancing across the plain. His great rivals—Mick Fanning, Taj Burrow, Joel Parkinson, and Andy Irons—are gone. Jordy Smith and Dane Reynolds briefly stepped into the firing line, and then the Brazilian storm of Gabriel Medina, Filipe Toledo, and Italo Ferreira exploded, vaporizing everything in its path. John John Florence has been the stellar performer of the last few years, with young Aussie Ethan Ewing just stepping into the fray. All of them are one or two generations removed from Kelly, a chasm apart.

Life has changed for Kelly now with a baby on the way with his longtime partner Kalani Miller and a formal retirement announcement…although a short time later he was back competing again at Teahupoo, and still beating some of the world's best with an age-defying performance. It was the world's shortest retirement. Why is Kelly still doing it, with almost everyone he knew long gone? What keeps him motivated after fifty-six wins and $2.2 million in prize money? What keeps him going, year after year, contest after contest, when he has seemingly nothing left to prove?

He still has that intense desire to win, to show he's still up there with the best. That fire, he freely admits, doesn't burn quite as fiercely as before. But he still wants to progress and improve. For Kelly, surfing great isn't the methodical process of beating an opponent but rather a deep desire to show the world how good he really is—he clearly doesn't define his surfing by contest scores but by his own impossibly high internal standard, and he seems determined to keep raising that standard. And he is searching for new inspiration.

Kelly has a genuine enthusiasm for the surfing, a red-hot burning stoke, and after incalculable success, new challenges are what Kelly and our sport need—surfing needs a revolution, and revolution doesn't come in increments. Some years back in late February, in the parking lot at Rincon Beach, with dusk trickling over the Santa Ynez Mountains, Kelly drives up in a dark truck

*Kelly Slater in 2014 at Teahupoo at the Billabong Pro Tahiti. Courtesy of World Surf League. Photo by Tom Servais.*

and jumps out, excitedly showing me one of his brand-new four-fin boards. At this stage, he is still unsure whether he will surf them in the pro contests coming up in Australia, but he says to me, "Hey, Shaun, I gotta make you one. I reckon five-foot-six will do it for you." I laugh—I last rode a five-foot-six four decades ago. He is genuinely stoked on the new board, stoked to make one for a fellow surfer. He gives no sense of being jaded with a brand-new year on tour approaching, just a stoked forever-young grommet with a new board, laughing with his young pal, running down the path to get some waves before the light fades.

Watching him sprint down the path, it's easy to see what keeps him going, what keeps him competing and progressing, what keeps his surfing young and vital. He is stoked, pure and simple, and for surfing's sake I hope he stays that way. We need him. We need him to keep coming up with crazy designs, we need him to keep risking his life at Teahupoo and Pipe, we need him to keep breaking records, and we need him to keep inspiring us.

Kelly tells me his best surfing experience was not winning a contest or the world title but a nighttime surf session with his old buddy Shane Dorian, at Restaurants on Tavarua Island, Fiji, pulling into phosphorescent barrels together on soft boards, lights strapped to their waists, watched by a group of shrieking Fijians.

"It was so bright you could see your reflection and your shadow on the reef. We surfed from ten till midnight, and after a couple of waves, we started riding doubles together. I had a waterproof light strapped onto my waist, and we're literally both pulling into the barrels on the same wave together, holding each other's rails, nose riding. And I swear, it sounds like I was doing acid or something, but I guarantee you I wasn't. But we looked up; there was a huge ring around the cloud that filled almost half the sky. There were just the two of us in the water, and we just surfed all night, and it was just epic. I mean, we're singing songs from the eighties, and it was a special moment in my life for sure."

In this complex world of ours, where we are always thinking, calculating, planning, and analyzing, it is reassuring to know that for us surfers, hidden inside the tube is a simple place where we can let our instincts take over, where we can react rather than plan. It is a rare refuge where we are truly disconnected from the confusion of the world, from our cell phones, social media, and computers. This is where Kelly Slater lives, in the moment, in a world of flow, where sensations are sharpened, the immediacy of life is brought into focus, and all that matters is to reach for the light that is shining ahead, pulled along by an invisible hand, absolutely and unequivocally confident that it will take him to where he needs to be.

*Kelly Slater in 2011 at Huntington Beach, California at the U.S. Open of Surfing. Courtesy of World Surf League. Photo by Jimmy "Jimmicane" Wilson*

# AFTERWORD

## TO SURF & PROTECT

Every surfer in the world can close their eyes and visualize a perfect wave. The surface is glassy, and the wave is breaking down the line quickly and steadily. The wave is steep and barrelling with the wind rushing up its face, creating a light, iridescent spray as the lip curls and cascades over. It may break like that for sixty seconds if it's an extraordinarily long wave, although most waves typically last less than fifteen seconds.

Each surfer in this book has a unique story, a journey of a lifetime dedicated to these fleeting moments, to finding and riding their own version of the perfect wave. For those of us fortunate enough to have found them, those precious few seconds of transcendence are seared into our minds forever. One of the things that makes the experience of surfing so special is that those moments, like a flickering flame, are ephemeral and can never be repeated again. That unique energy signature, that confluence of specific meteorological conditions—you can never ride the same wave twice, and truly great surfable waves are exceedingly rare.

There are approximately 1.5 million miles of coastline in the world, with waves breaking on them about 8,600 times every day, and yet good surfing waves are very uncommon, and world-class waves are so scarce that most surfers know their names and locations by heart. It takes a perfect set of geomorphic, oceanographic, and meteorological circumstances to align to create a great wave. First, you need energy from a storm to create a consistent swell over the open ocean. Then that swell must be bent, focused, and then broken in just such a way to create a wave that breaks and peels along its crest at a perfect speed (not too fast, not too slow), with a steepness that accelerates the surfer, maybe even steep enough to break over the surfer and form a tube. The wind must be calm or light offshore, and the tide must be just right. Some waves do this somewhat consistently, others seasonally, and others only on very rare occasions.

Great surfing waves are incredibly sensitive to change. Changes in the bottom topography, modifications to the shore, loss of sediment supply, or offshore structures can all impact the quality of waves, sometimes for the better (e.g., the Wedge), but most often for the worse (e.g., Killer Dana). Not to mention impacts from polluted water or the ability to access them by the public. Further, I would argue that surfing in a wild, healthy ocean and communing with nature enhances the overall experience. Even better, every wave on the planet is a public commons—nobody owns them, and they are a natural resource for everyone to share and enjoy.

Given their rarity and sensitivity, all great surfing waves should be the UNESCO World Heritage sites of surfing (great surfing waves deserve that designation!) and should be protected as such. Sadly, many of our favorite surfing waves are threatened by water pollution, loss of access, alteration of the shoreline, and climate change, including loss of coral, sea level rise, and increased storm severity.

Beyond surfing the waves themselves, most surfers genuinely love the ocean, the beach, and their coastal communities. And because surfers spend more time immersed in the ocean than any other group, they're also more likely to suffer the effects of a polluted ocean, and to understand the threats our oceanic and coastal environments face intimately. For these reasons, all surfers, by their very nature, should inherently be coastal conservation advocates. As should we all—our ocean needs to be protected and preserved.

If the three-million-plus surfers in the US and tens of millions worldwide united in their love and passion for the ocean and took collective action, we could be an unstoppable force for ocean and coastal conservation.

We have a long way to go to see that happen, so I encourage you to channel your passion and love of surfing into action. Together, we can ensure that those perfect waves seared into your mind are around for the next generation of surfers.

For our ocean, waves, and beaches,

—*Dr. Chad Nelsen*
CEO Surfrider Foundation

### About the Surfrider Foundation

*The Surfrider Foundation is a nonprofit grassroots organization dedicated to the protection and enjoyment of our world's ocean, waves, and beaches for all people through a powerful activist network. Founded in 1984 by a handful of visionary surfers in Malibu, California, the Surfrider Foundation now maintains over one million supporters, activists, and members, with more than 200 volunteer-led chapters and student clubs in the US, and more than 800 victories protecting our coasts.*
**Learn more at surfrider.org.**

*Michael February in 2021 at Dunes, Kommetjie, South Africa. Photo by Alan van Gysen*